GW00836671

Stop Being a F***ing Idiot

Orlando Winters

BWM Press LLC
Miami, Florida

Orlando Winters
boywritesmiami.com

First Printing: January 2013
BWM Press LLC

ISBN 0-615-74787-6
ISBN-13 978-0615747873

For my lovely Dana.

Because I'm sure there's no sweeter gift
than a collection of profanity-laced nonsense.

I'm dedicating the book's completion to you.
Not the content.

Thanks for putting up with me.

CONTENTS

INTRODUCTION

If anything in this book is inaccurate, blame it on science. I do my best to avoid being a fucking idiot, but occasionally the nature of science makes it such that when one thing is accepted as fact, new evidence comes forth to blow your previous assumptions out of the water. Granted, it's rare for something to completely change an established fact rather than just modify it, but it does happen. For example, long ago when racism existed it was thought that a white person could not receive a blood transfusion from a black person. I don't know how this started, because I didn't exist; however, it was likely started by a bunch of uppity white people, or black people who were pissed that the whites already took their rights and dignity, and didn't want them to siphon their blood as well. Either way, this was *fact* to most people. Was this regarded as fact in the scientific community? Probably not. I need a better example.

Pluto was once considered a planet. This was a scientific fact, and you know it's a scientific fact when schools teach a nifty mnemonic in order to remember it. "My Very Educated Mother Just Served Us Nine Pizzas" is the one I recall best since it made the grossly counterfactual assumption that my mother was both educated and irresponsible enough as a parent to force-feed us an exorbitant amount of pizza. It was a staple of most of our childhoods: Pluto is a planet. Then, in 2006, some asshole scientists decided that Pluto was, in fact, not a planet. This revelation occurred because there were many other objects similar to Pluto discovered in the late 20th and early 21st centuries, some of which were even larger.

Scientists were faced with two choices: add a bunch of new planets to the point where schoolchildren are being taught mnemonics longer than *Atlas Shrugged*, or codify what a planet is. It turns out that prior to 2006, there was no concrete definition of what a planet was. We were just finding shit orbiting the Sun and, if it was big and roundish enough, gave it a name that didn't look like a UPS tracking number and got a bunch of rocket scientists to throw a probe at it. Thanks to this new definition, we now know that Pluto is not a planet, but a "dwarf planet." When this fact changed, we weren't automatically fucking idiots for having believed Pluto was a planet, and midgets felt a sting knowing that adding the word "dwarf" to anything suddenly made it that much shittier.

In 2009, the state of Illinois decided that Pluto would be reinstated as a planet—in Illinois. So everywhere else in the known universe, Pluto isn't a planet, but in Illinois it is.

Those Illinois lawmakers are fucking idiots, and that's the kind of person who this book is about. By the way, thanks for buying it; "I'll use the money wisely," said the author facetiously.

CHAPTER 1
Confidence!

> *"No one can make you feel inferior*
> *without your consent."*
> —Eleanor Roosevelt

Try this quick exercise: walk up to the very first stranger you see, and tell them a joke. Here, I'll give you one.

Q: What's brown and rhymes with "Snoop"?
A: Dr. Dre.

Did you do it? Of course not, because you're a pussy. Confident people command respect. Confident people can say just a few words and garner everyone's attention. Confident people are also, for the most part, full of shit.

I'm a confident person. I didn't always used to be, but now I am. How did I do it? The same way the Iraq War was started: by fooling every fucking person under the sun! The advice "fake it 'till you make it" is one of the most useful little rhymes I know, besides "he who smelt it, dealt it."

In high school, I was in the marching band. If that's not enough, I was a tall (6'2"), lanky, pimply geek weighing in at around 140 pounds fully-clothed. Genes are assholes. Taking all that into account, I had the self-awareness to realize that if I wanted to get laid, it would require either being molested by a teacher or relying on the charisma I had approximately zero of. So I started emulating the cool guys. At first I was scared shitless, because I figured it would only be a matter of time before people realized a concentration camp stand-in such as myself couldn't possibly be that confident. However, a funny thing happened. People started buying it. I would tell jokes, and people would laugh. I'd talk to girls, acting calm and collected while in my mind I was this cold little naked child crying in a corner—yet they'd flirt back. Everything started getting more and more awesome. I got myself a girlfriend (who wouldn't fuck me, but whatever, dude, baby steps) and one day I realized that, holy shit, I'm starting to feel confident.

Faking confidence eventually led to being perceived by others as confident, and this in turn made me as cocksure as I needed to be. Just like that. I mean, I'm still a geek, but the confidence I employ when I pull out my pocket watch (yes) is unrivaled.

Becoming a more confident individual doesn't necessitate changing who you are. Are you shy? You can, as strange as it sounds, be both shy and confident. The opposite of shyness isn't confidence, it's assertiveness. Yes, I know "assertive" is probably the first-listed synonym for "confident," but you know what? Fuck you, and fuck your thesaurus. You can be shy and confident; I've met many people who hold that title. My point is, you don't need to change your whole personality, just that shitty part that makes you unsure of your shit.

Don't mix confidence with arrogance, though, because that'll turn you into an asshole. The only time you can acceptably act arrogantly is if your sense of humor can shield you from your perceived assholery, and that's no trivial task. It's best to just avoid arrogance altogether; otherwise, you'll have to actually be the best at something so no one calls you on your bluff. And, let's face it, you're probably not the best at anything. Wayne Gretzky was the best hockey player. Muhammad Ali was the best boxer. I thought I was the best in my 4th-grade class's spelling bee until some little Asian chick spelled "loquacious." I didn't even know what the fuck that word meant. Even rereading that word now, I still think it's a black girl's name.

So what are the attributes of a confident person? There are many, I'm sure, but these are mine: Be your own person, and don't find the need to validate who you are. Believe in your abilities. Don't fear someone's opinion of you, i.e., don't walk into a room thinking everyone is judging you, because they likely aren't (they're too worried about themselves). If you have something to say, fucking say it and don't be timid about it.

I'm serious, man. Out of all the things I'm about to say in this book, this is the most important. Confidence is the key to improving all social aspects of your life, be it business or pleasure. Fake that shit until you make it. Now, go tell a stranger a fucking joke.

CHAPTER 2

Know Your Audience.

"Cleveland fans are awesome."
—LeBron James

If you're still reading at this point, that means I know my audience, and thus the book gains credibility. Some people are assertive, some are shy, some are intellectual, and some are Russian. As I've said before, you don't need to change who you are to make friends or influence people.

You just need to pick the right people to be friends with.

That may sound like pretext, like something that doesn't quite address the crux of the problem, but think about it logically for a second. How the fuck does a Japanese businessman get along with an inner-city amateur rapper-slash-urban-pharmacist? Where do they find common ground? They don't, that's how. Except in action-comedy movies.

Look at all the bullshit I write. Would you consider it wise for me to write copy for church pamphlets? No, because that's not my audience. The kind of people who read churchly writings wouldn't find it humorous of me to refer to Jesus as "that magical Jew with a posse." I don't know if you've ever received hate mail from Christians, but holy shit, most church services don't quote the Bible as much as those people do. One message I received said, "Matthew 15:11—It is not what goes into the mouth that defiles a person, but what comes out of the mouth; this defiles a person." Fellatio jokes would've been too easy, so I opted for replying with, "Well, technically, none of that came out of my mouth, since I typed it." A couple of email exchanges later I decided it was futile, so I stopped.

Not everyone is going to like you. (Even Queen Elizabeth II, the sweet old lady that she is, still has a bunch of pissed-off anarchists seething with hatred of her and everyone in her lineage.) Accept that fact and move forward. I know people with a pathological need to be liked by everyone they come into contact with. I tell each of them the same thing, "If you somehow manage to defy the nature of humanity and get everyone you ever meet to like you, I swear on Zeus's beard I will hate you. I will hate you with a flaming passion that burns hotter than something really, really hot, which I can't think of right now."

I'm not being an asshole; I'm just trying to inject some reality into their fantasy. Some personalities just don't mix. Accept it. The best route to take in this situation is the one that lets you avoid those people. If you're a stone-cold, gay-loving, pro-choice, anti-gun, whatever-other-thing liberal, don't fucking talk about political views with a conservative unless that's your job or it's some sort of progressive fraternity hazing I've never heard of.

Are you afraid that maybe you have no audience, because you've always been a bit of an outcast and considered weird by everyone you come into contact with? Let me tell you, you're not alone. There's a niche for everything. There are black neo-Nazis. Some guys like fingering their pee holes, and objects are sold online to suit that purpose. Vegans are a thing. No matter how weird or "unique" you think you are, no matter how out-there your secret is, there is a blog dedicated to it. Rule 34 of the

Internet states: "If it exists, there is porn of it." So not only does your weirdness definitely exist out there to some capacity, there are also people who masturbate to your quirkiness. You hear that? You being a doll-house-filled-with-dead-roaches aficionado turns someone on.

There would be a lot less turmoil in the world if people just avoided those they can't get along with wherever possible.

CHAPTER 3

Learn to Take a Hint.

"It is no use trying to sum people up.
One must follow hints,
not exactly what is said,
nor yet entirely what is done."
—John Greenleaf Whittier or Virginia Woolfe
(the Internet is unreliable)

In elementary school I was positively smitten over a girl in my class named Clarissa. She was so pretty, and I made sure I professed my love for her every chance I got. I called her names, I put a lizard in her hair, and I made her run away crying— twice! How could that little bitch not understand how much I cared about her?

The most common language in the world isn't Chinese, English, or whatever it is Indian people speak. It's body language. Maybe you cringed at that terrible pun, but it's true. If you ever want to take a hint from someone, ignore what they say and focus on what they do. Understanding context cues is paramount. "No, stop!" can have a completely different meaning than usual if, for example, you agreed on a safe word beforehand.

I don't really have time to go on about the intricacies of body language, because it's a more in-depth field than one would suspect and beyond the scope of this book. It's worth taking the time to read up on it from credible sources—there's a lot of crap out there.

There are some clues that are obvious, like someone crossing their arms and shaking their head after you ask them if they'd like to smell your finger. Others require a bit more perceptiveness. For example, when someone in a meeting rests their chin on their hand while covering their mouth with their fingers, it means they think your idea is stupid as shit but doesn't want to tell you.

Body language is remarkably powerful and often overlooked. People tend to forget that we're animals, and animals have "tells" that give away their feelings. A dog will put its tail between its legs when it's scared, a cat's ears will angle back when threatened, and Tom Cruise will flip his shit and jump on Oprah's couch when he's in love. Women pick up on that sort of thing better than men do, which is why guys tend to get caught doing stupid things all the time, because their body language gives them away.

In some cases, what people say is all you have to go on, so you have to read into things a little differently and try to decipher what it is they're implying, rather than the things they seem to be explicitly saying.

To give you a firm example, think of Enrique Iglesias. He produces amazingly awful music. I've battled through some heavy-duty post-traumatic stress disorder (my psychiatrist is still billing me) after hearing him "sing" one of his shitty songs. The guy sounds like a deaf person learning to cry. In Enrique's music, he says a lot of things that, if taken at face value, means he wants to rape you. He's got a song titled *Finally Found You*, which is about him finally finding his latest victim and the things he yells at her across a dark alley. I wanted to break down the lyrics and show you why it screams "aggravated assault and sexual misconduct," but it didn't make the editing process. Apparently, I would have to pay permission rights to do so, and there's no way in hell I'm paying Enrique Iglesias to let me make fun of him. Instead, I'll paraphrase to circumvent the law, the same way he circumvents disturbance laws by calling his nonsensical screaming "singing."

"Girl, I'm gonna get you"
"I don't care what I have to do, I'll do it"
"Your friends don't give a shit about you"
"If they try to find you, I'll hide you in a crowd"
"I've been looking for a rape victim for ages"
"Get in the fucking van"
"Seriously, bitch, get in the van, I have a gun"

In my head, I could hear the girl crying frantically as she tries to get away from Enrique's grasp. She's sobbing, her mascara is running, and behind her is this Latin heartthrob unbuttoning the only button he ever buttons on his fucking shirt as he corners her and begins to unzip his leather pants. It's horrible. Seriously, try saying—not singing—any of those things next time you're at a club and want to talk to a pretty lady. Unless you've built up a sizable tolerance to getting your ass kicked by bouncers and white knights, I wish you luck.

The reason Enrique gets away with that shit is twofold. One, it's a dance song. Songwriters aren't expected to write intelligent lyrics for idiots gyrating to a style of music known for calling women bitches and otherwise using ninety-eight percent of the song's run time to explain how much better the artists are than you, and the other two percent to say their own name. And two, what he's actually doing is hinting at consensual sex with some girl, not abduction and rape. He just chose his words poorly.

Paying attention to what people are trying to tell you goes beyond just listening to their words verbatim. Master it, and you'll immediately be viewed as less of a moron. Don't master it, and that barista you keep staring at every morning is going to file a restraining order on you.

CHAPTER 4

Nobody Likes Drama Queens.

"I CAN'T BELIEVE THIS SHIT!"
—Some fucking idiot's ambiguous status update

Can you guess what the most accurate litmus test for determining a person's drama queen status is? The phrase "I hate drama" comes to mind. You never hear a level-headed, sane person state the obvious, the same way you never hear them say, "I hate being waterboarded."

Some people thrive on drama, and in many instances they're completely oblivious to that fact, along with the reality that they generally create it. When something happens, it's the worst fucking thing in the world. Not only is it unimaginably terrible in their minds, but oftentimes they won't elaborate. Oh, they'll make their displeasure known throughout the land; however, they'll follow up any inquiries with, "I don't want to talk about it." (Apparently they signed a non-disclosure agreement with their psychosis.) I call these people "reality thespians."

Reality thespians prosper with attention, like plants. Really shitty plants. At some point in their lives they learned that the best way to receive attention was to whine like an asshole. Making a case out of any little unfavorable event is the realm of children. Next time you see a baby, take its candy. It's going to start to cry like a little bitch. Try the same thing with an adult. Most adults will just be like, "Dude, give it back," but the drama queens will piss and moan, tweet it, Instagram it, post it on their Facebook walls, vlog about it on YouTube, and start a Tumblr blog about it called "thisguytookmycandy.tumblr.com." They'll update said blog with photos they find of you superimposed with bold, red text with captions like, "LITERALLY HITLER."

These irrational human clusterfucks are impervious to rational discourse. Here's precisely what they lack: prudence.

Mark Twain said a lot of cool shit, though some of it was quasi-racist. But beyond that, he once said, "You can't reason someone out of something they weren't reasoned into." If your run-of-the-mill reality thespian can't give you a valid mental analysis of why they feel the need to write haiku in blood in a dark room someplace, you won't be doing any convincing today.

When other people are drama queens, they are easy to spot because they operate in extremes. Every comment they're given is either the nicest thing they've ever heard, or the most fucked up, innocence-raping vitriol ever divulged.

But recognizing your own inner-reality thespian is a whole other ball game. Here's a quiz: Do most people know twice as much about you as you know about them? Do complete strangers know things about you they didn't want to know? Have you ever simultaneously laughed and cried while not pregnant or menstruating? When telling a story, are you a more hardcore method actor than Christian Bale as you gesticulate wildly and act out scenes? I'll let you evaluate your own responses.

Let's set up a typical scenario. I crumple up a flyer from some Occupy Whatever shit a dirty hippie just handed me and toss it in the trash as if I were a basketball player. It accidentally hits a girl standing next to the trash bin. She flips the fuck out, I apologize, and I continue on with my day. For me, the event finalizes. For her, life as she knows it has collapses around her in a sea of cascading conundrums. You see, because that little paper hits her ever-so-slightly on the elbow, she has to tweet about it. Her boyfriend sees the location tag and notices she lied to him about her whereabouts during their phone conversation a few minutes prior, so he inquires about that. She flips out, accusing him of accusing her of cheating. Quickly, the fight escalates and she asks for a break in their relationship. That night she goes home, and being the stress eater she is (a trait she acquired from her neurotic father, according to her) she gorges on ice cream. This behavior continues for weeks, and once her boyfriend realizes how obese she's getting, he decides to end their relationship. And then she proclaims it's all my fucking fault.

If this sounds anything like you, stop. If at any point in that story you called her boyfriend an asshole or sympathized with her in any way, stop. If you're still hung up on the title of this book and find it a personal affront, for the love of God, stop.

CHAPTER 5

It's OK to Curse.

"When you use a curse word, it means you are not educated enough to substitute that word with another."
—Some fucking idiot

FUCK A SHIT COCK.

People experience a disconnect when it comes to profanity. They believe certain words hold a precise, arcane power. That's the original root of what a curse word is. It's in the fucking name: "curse." People believed that when they uttered specific words, their boldness brought curses upon the recipient. That antiquated mindset has remained pervasive throughout the centuries to the point that when a child says "fuck," they get scolded or smacked by the very parents who taught them that word and hypocritically use it behind their backs. Their excuse is that the child is too young to use the word. Get the fuck out of here, it's a word, not a cock ring.

The word itself means nothing; it's the implication. I can say "fuck" while laughing to denote something is surprisingly pleasing, or with a whimsically puzzling look to tell everyone something is tricky, or I can grimace and yell it in pain. None of those should in any way offend anyone, because the word isn't being used in offensive context. If I say "fuck you" angrily, the meaning is clear. Now suppose I replace the word "fuck" with the word "fudge." It's perfectly acceptable to say on TV, and yet the implication remains exactly the same—the only difference is I sound like a tool. I'm letting you know that the current situation between us is unfavorable. In this context, both mean the exact same thing. I just granted "fudge" the identical level of power as "fuck," and somehow that's OK. Why? Because idiots. If you want to get rid of the perceived meaning of curse words, you'll have to get rid of the feelings which bring their use, and that's not going to happen.

Communicative vulgarity isn't relegated to language; it's all about context and implication. The phrase "Fuck you, douche bag, eat my shit," said in anger, is vulgar and dismissive. If we replace those words with "Away with you, wretched scoundrel, and masticate my excrement," it makes it sound classier, but I'm still telling you to fuck off. So the argument against cursing is what, that you prefer a more archaic prose when someone tells you to chew their poop? If what I'm implying is inherently mean in nature, why does it matter the words I use to describe it? Why does that make it more acceptable? If you're worried about dumbing down the language, start by cracking down on rappers, and while you're at it, build a time machine and beat a dude named William Shakespeare to death.

I'm not equating the use of profanity with Shakespeare (even though he wrote a lot of bawdy shit), but if the problem is the use of certain words when other words will do, then Shakespeare shouldn't be as revered as he is. Are you sick and tired of the way rappers these days throw out the word "swag" randomly and speak of how much swagger they have? Shakespeare must've been the original Soulja Boy Tell 'Em, because he coined that fucking word. He invented a shitload of words, some *obscene*, some *worthless*, but to this day it's *fashionable* to use them. I *bet* you don't know which words he coined, but I'll give you a *hint*—it's over 1,700 of them. If Shakespeare were to curse at you and you derided him for it, he'd have promptly told you to go fuck yourself in a phrase he made up which youths will make themselves millionaires from parroting some 400 years later.

The imbecilic argument that using a curse word means you're too uneducated to substitute that word with another, less colorful one is equally inane. You can apply that to anything. If you said, "Today I bought a vibrator" you're clearly an uneducated buffoon, because you should've said, "I purchased an oscillating pleasure apparatus this day." They mean the same goddamn thing, and no one fucking talks like that, except maybe on *Dawson's Creek* where all those teen wordsmiths made me watch television with a thesaurus. There's a quote: "Brevity is the soul of wit." I don't know who said that, but he was witty as fuck. Oh, sorry: "I know not who speaketh that passage, however his repartee was unrivaled." It would be fun if everyone spoke like that, but no one does. Last time I used the word "perhaps," I got called a faggot for a week.

There's no need to be uppity about the use of a curse word. Seriously now, fuck that shit.

CHAPTER 6

Never Be Easily Offended.

"Sticks and stones may break my bones,
but words will never hurt me."
—Some fucking genius

The Holocaust never happened.

You probably just got offended as shit, and for that I apologize. That was an example of something that is understandably offensive, unless it were said by Sacha Baron Cohen doing one of his ironically racist characters. I'm not an anti-Semite, I'm actually quite pro-Semite. Not pro-Semite to the point where I'm like, "Fuck yeah, Jews, you can do no wrong," but pro-Semite to where a person being Jewish is of absolutely no consequence to me, except for my taking the occasional playful stereotype at their expense. This book is also intended to be humorous, regardless of what some little shit giving a negative review may lead you to believe. Knowing that, and understanding what my intention is, and that Jews are awesome, you shouldn't be offended by the horseshit statement that the Holocaust never happened. I know for a fact it happened, because I had a college professor who was there. Not "there" there; he was born in 1944 in Broken Arrow, Oklahoma. However, he once claimed having a spiritual journey to a concentration camp while tripping balls on peyote. That dude was the best music teacher I ever had, so I believe him.

There's nothing wrong with being offended. If you're trying to bury your eighteen-year-old son who was killed in a war zone halfway across the world and some assholes picket the funeral holding up "God Hates Fags" and "Your Son Will Burn In Hell" signs, not only do you have a right to be offended, but you should be legally entitled to challenge one of those protesters to a fun little gentleman's duel. I don't know how much reading you do, but a gentleman's duel involves two guys shooting at each other from a couple of yards away. That's probably the extent of learning I experienced watching Bugs Bunny cartoons as a child. That, and how coyotes have unprecedented amounts of disposable income.

On the other hand, there is a huge problem with being *easily* offended. If a couple of gay guys want to throw the gayest, most fabulous wedding of all time, the only way it should offend you is if you weren't invited. The food would probably be spectacular. Even so, people are offended by gays marrying. Why the fuck.

I've found this increasingly difficult to comprehend: why would anyone want to make something (that has nothing to do with them) their problem? There are people somewhere in the world right now who actively enjoy shitting on each other's chest. They enjoy it. I think it's disgusting, but I'm not about to make it my problem. If they want to deal with the smell, mess, and logistical nightmare of getting the poop off their chest and into a toilet, let them. I'll have no part of it, and up until I wrote this I didn't even think about it.

One time I was wearing a pair of bright yellow pants at my best friend's bachelor party. The pants were my girlfriend's idea, possibly to disarm women into thinking me a homosexual, but that's irrelevant right now. I was walking down the street when some car full of the most dubious of ruffians slow-creeped up next to me. One guy yells, "FUCK YELLOW." Serious psychological issues aside, the dude was trying me. Someone who is easily offended would yell some shit back or let it ruin his night. I laughed, because it was funny, and let it go. That's what you need to do with stupid shit. Just let it go.

Imagine for a second that they stopped at a red light and I run up to the car. I yell at the guy, he steps out of the car, we shove each other a bit, he takes a swing at me, I swing back and clock him in the jaw. Then he falls over and his neck hits the fender, breaking his spine and killing him. I get prison time for manslaughter, and the inmates call me "Unmellow Yellow." Probably the best name they could come up with. They're not scholars, they're prisoners. All that shit because I got easily offended. Obviously, that's up there in unlikely, worst-case scenarios, but that sort of thing has happened before. A more realistic version could've been getting into a fight with the guy and having the everliving shit kicked out of me, since I fight like a disoriented mental patient. That would be fucking stupid.

Being easily offended makes you the asshole no one likes to hang around, because everyone has to watch what they say. Either that or you hang around other easily-offended assholes and form a club. Next thing you know, you're picketing soldier funerals.

CHAPTER 7

Don't Play the Lottery.

> *"You can't win if you don't play."*
> —Some fucking idiot

Understanding the concept of odds and probabilities is fairly straightforward, yet it's amazing how some people manage to rightly fuck that up.

Take the lottery.

People play the lottery all the time unaware of how mind-bogglingly difficult it is to win. It seems like they take a different approach to probabilities. Their rationale must be, "Well, I can either win it or not win it, so my odds of winning are 50/50."

Obviously, that's stupid. The reality is a bit more "fuck you" than that. Making up a lottery here, let's say you're supposed to choose five numbers between 1 and 50. The odds of winning are 1 in 2,118,760. Those are what we call "terrible odds." Real lotteries with massive payouts give you even more brain-fucking odds. There are popular lotteries which give chances around the 1 in 175,223,510 mark. Those numbers molest the eyes. Chipping away at the veneer that helps psychologically frame those odds as more accessible (for example, believing "I only have to guess a number between 1 and 59 a few times!"), it becomes apparent that hitting the jackpot isn't going to fucking happen to you. What 1 in 175 million means is being asked to choose a number from 1 to 175,223,510.

Go ahead, choose a number and turn to the next page to see if you've won.

You didn't fucking win, idiot.

I don't subscribe to any sort of psychology-related newsletters or anything, but I've been known to pick up a phrase or two from the Internet. One of those phrases is *availability bias* and it explains why people delude themselves into thinking they could win the lottery. There's probably more psychobabble bullshit to it, but essentially it's the tendency to judge probabilities based on how easily examples come to mind.

Quick demonstration: You're taking a multiple choice test and the Asian kid you're cheating off of answers "B" for question five. A couple of seconds later he pauses, looks it over and squints (or at least you think he's squinting—you can't really tell), and he changes the answer from "B" to "D." Based on the multiple times you've been told over the years by various teachers and know-it-all assholes, you'd leave it as "B," because "If in doubt, stick with your first answer."

Bullshit. Over 33 different studies since 1970 have shown that not only are the assholes wrong, but you end up doing better when you go against your gut if you're in doubt. This is because of availability bias. The times you changed your answer and got it wrong mentally outweigh the times you got it right. It's the same reason why people are afraid of getting killed by a shark, even though more people die from horse-related injuries every year. I say "horse-related," because that includes being fucked to death by a horse. Yes, it has happened numerous times.

To overcome availability bias, just think it through. How many people do you know who have *not* been killed by a shark? How many people played the lottery last week and *didn't* hit the jackpot? I know of at least fourteen people who haven't been killed by sharks; the rest, I would have to ask them. You're right, you "could" win the lottery, but I'll be right the 175,223,509 times that you lost out of the 175,223,510 times you played.

If you play the lottery because spending a buck or two every once in a while for hope and the opportunity to dream a little bit is worth it to you, that's fine. If you habitually play it week after week, thinking your turn is coming up any day now, please pick a number from 1 to 175,223,510. And send me a dollar when you lose, idiot.

CHAPTER 8

Don't Believe in Superstitions.

"If you open an umbrella indoors, it's bad luck!"
—Some fucking idiot

My girlfriend and I once discussed superstitions. I stated that there are some superstitions that are more retarded than others, and she countered by saying they were all equally as absurd. She has a point, but I maintain that some are extra moronic.

There's a superstition about how you shouldn't walk under a ladder, lest you be destined for bad luck. Exactly how long this bad luck lasts is a matter open to debate, but let's go with twelve. You're probably thinking, "Twelve what?" Exactly. It doesn't make any fucking sense. However, when invoking common sense, walking under a ladder isn't the brightest thing to do for multiple reasons. You could get your shirt caught on it and rip it, or perhaps bump into a shaky ladder and have an object fall on you, or you could be in the worst fraternity ever and walking under a ladder means the guy on top of it unloads his bowels while the rest of the fuckers have a good laugh at your expense. The point is, it's generally a bad idea to walk under a ladder to begin with, so one could argue that the bad luck potential is present regardless. It's still stupid, but it's less irrational than tossing salt over your shoulder because of a minor salt spill.

Skipping cracks on a sidewalk is fun, but I'm not allowed to do it without having you fucking dickheads judge me. People will assume I'm superstitious, and while I do care about my mother's spine, I don't believe for a second that walking on an old sidewalk will sentence my mom to a wheelchair. Otherwise, angsty teens everywhere would be extorting their parents for higher allowances by hovering over pavement. Maybe the bold ones would graze the crack ever so slightly, giving their mothers scoliosis to show they mean business, I don't know. Kids are fucking assholes. I once poured out a new bottle of cooking oil and peed in it hoping to trick someone into frying things in my piss. Never mind that the consistency of oil and a five-year-old's urine could be told apart by even the most novice of chefs; I just wanted to watch the world burn.

Most superstitions violate causality harder than most cops violate traffic laws. What, you broke a mirror? Well, I hope you like bad luck, because the universe really, really loves mirrors and hates making sense. How in the everliving fuck does the number thirteen in a building equal evil? Are owners of black cats living in perpetual misfortune?

No. Like ugly Asian babies, valid superstitions don't exist. At best, any perceived effect of a superstition is you merely psyching yourself out. Think of it as an asshole placebo.

I went on a long road trip once and started playing Nintendo 3DS. It was a terrible choice to focus my eyes on a tiny 3D screen in a moving vehicle, but I suppose I momentarily forgot a deal I made with Father Time wherein I provided my youthful constitution in exchange for a 401k and a slowly receding hairline. My stomach started feeling uneasy and I began having a slight headache. I've felt this way before, it goes away after about fifteen to twenty minutes of stopping the activity that put me in that state. But someone in the car told me about this wonderful remedy/superstition involving gripping a rock for dear life to make the pain go away. "Um…" I asked. She replied, "It works, trust me." So I held her rock for a few seconds and told her it wasn't working. "You need to hold it for a while and it'll make you feel better."

Guess how long I had to hold it? Fifteen to twenty fucking minutes. Isn't that an amazing goddamn coincidence? Those kinds of superstitions are harmless, though. Very stupid, very useless, but mostly harmless. The ones that put you at some point past fucking idiot are the ones that do very real harm.

Show any kid anywhere a picture of a rhino and ask them if they think it's cool. Of course they'll say yes, because rhinos are fucking awesome. They're the closest thing we've got to unicorns, and when they poop they wave their tail in a way that spreads their projectile feces in many directions. I knew a guy like that once, minus the tail part, and he would shit everywhere, all the time. He called it "irritable bowel syndrome," but I called it "hilarious." Anyway, the Sumatran rhino has nearly gone extinct because a long time ago a bunch of Chinese medicine men claimed rhino horn shavings cured everything from snakebites to "devil possession." It's not used to make dicks hard, as many claim, but with all the random shit they're alleging rhino horns do, we might as well add that to the list. This supposition more than likely arose from a combination of hogwash and time naturally healing a wound while they tried different things, with rhino horn being last, as symptoms began to subside. They employed faulty logic, attributing the resolution of the symptoms (caused naturally, by the body's own defenses) to the last thing they tried. If they had toyed with rubbing hobo semen on their heads at that particular time instead of rhino horn shavings, China would have the happiest bums in existence. Imagine all those Chinese nurses going alley to alley jacking off a bunch of schizophrenic vagabonds. Rhinos live, homeless dudes get off, and a whole new branch of fetish porn emerges in the West. Everybody wins.

So what's in these magical horns? Keratin, the same thing that makes human hair and human nails. Rhino horn has been tested multiple times and every single time was found to have no effect on the human body whatsoever. Even so, because of this superstition and fucking idiots everywhere, we're killing off all our big animals, working toward making sure the biggest, most awesome beast on the planet is the sloth. I'm not putting my future kids' sloth paintings on my fridge. Fuck that.

Quit it with the superstitions. They serve no purpose and make you look like a fucking idiot around those of us who don't subscribe to your brand of insanity.

CHAPTER 9

Faith Is Personal.

"Religion is like a penis. It's fine to have one and fine to be proud of it, but please don't whip it out in public and wave it around. And please don't try to shove it down my child's throat."

—Some fucking genius

Raise your hand if you love Mormons showing up at your house asking if they can speak to you about the Lord and Savior, Jesus Christ. Now, if you raised your hand, only keep it up if you did it to defy me. Dick.

I'm an atheist (agnostic), which means I don't believe in God, but at the same time I don't rule out the possibility—though not for a personal god. I'd rather not give a shit about the matter than be all ritualistic in an attempt to purportedly get into Heaven. Think about how you'd react if some guy were throwing an awesome party, but in order to get on the list you had to call up his assistant every once in a while and tell him every time you've cursed, wanted your neighbor's car, or thought about a different party. And you also had to tell everyone about this fucking narcissist and how amazing he is. There's no way you're going to go through with that, and that's for a party you know exists.

When I "came out" to my mother about my lack of faith, she was like, "Why couldn't your secret be that you're gay?" We don't get parades, awareness months, or public support. What we do get is scorn, judgment, and (apparently) a one-way ticket to Hell.

Some people wear their faith on their sleeves, and that's stupid. I suppose their excuse is they're proud of it. I'm proud of my well-shaped ball sack, but I don't make it a goddamn talking point. If you want to believe in a personal god, by all means, praise the Lord! However, before you go praising the Lord in other people's faces, think about how annoyed you'd be if others were constantly trying to convert you to their religion. Christianity is like the Honda Civic of religions; it's pervasive. Followers aren't generally fighting off hordes of missionaries beyond the odd-Mormon here and there. Plus Christians are notorious for acting like used car salesmen, treating non-Christians as if they're standing there holding a blank check and sporting a hard-on for unreliable vehicles. Those are the same people who blow a gasket when someone says "Happy Holidays" instead of "Merry Christmas" and claim liberals declared war on Christmas. We liberals must have a shitty military, I guess, because we've yet to win said war.

Sending someone a prayer isn't what anyone would call meddling, so that's fine. I'm willing to bet most people who say things like "I'm praying for you in this time of need" don't actually go through with it anyway. Even if they do, prayers are just uttered words. If simply wishing for something to happen had any effect, anal prolapse would be a serious epidemic amongst most purveyors of pop music, thanks to me. Tabloids have yet to report Enrique Iglesias's rectum falling out of his body, so I'm pretty sure that, yeah, prayers are just uttered words.

Mark 16:15–16 says, "And he said to them, 'Go into all the

world and proclaim the gospel to the whole creation. Whoever believes and is baptized will be saved, but whoever does not believe will be condemned.' " Before the Internet, I guess that made sense, but you don't need to bring awareness anymore. Everyone's pretty aware. We're aware as fuck.

So let people be condemned in peace.

CHAPTER 10
Don't Be Xenophobic.

"They are twelve percent of the population, who cares?"

—Rush Limbaugh, some fucking idiot

The first time I heard the word "xenophobia," I honestly thought it meant the fear of the Xenomorph from the *Alien* movies. I later discovered it's still the fear of aliens, but of the brown variety. Or, you know, whatever breed isn't yours. As a kid in elementary school, I once asked a teacher why we call dogs that look different a "breed" even though they're the same species, while we call humans that look different "People with Down Syndrome." I didn't get an answer, but I did get detention, so I learned to never ask questions in class again.

All seriousness aside, prejudice is stupid. On the face of it, it seems fairly hypocritical of me to point that out, seeing as you can find the word "nigger" a few times in this book. First of all, I'm not calling anyone a nigger. Every time I've used that word it's to point out how you shouldn't use it, or like right now where I'm explaining myself. I'm not going to sugarcoat it and write "the N-word" because it's as stupid as blurring out a clear middle finger or bleeping out "f—k" where you crisply hear the F and the K. The point is, any sort of prejudice where you aren't directly being negatively affected by it is stupid. This includes all that shit: racism, classism, homophobia, and nearly everything else the ACLU positively jizz their collective trousers over.

I crack race-related jokes all the time; that's not the problem.

The problem comes in when you encroach upon other people's rights because your Southern great grandmother owned a human at one point, or because the thought of scissoring disgusts you. I find the premise of scissoring to be quite enchanting, personally, but even if I didn't, I wouldn't be going on about how terrible it is and how I don't want to raise my children in a world where a couple of lumberjack lesbians are allowed to rub labia in private.

Does it stem from fear? Possibly. Some people are intensely fearful that any outside change, anything different from their norm, is a threat to their status quo. If that's you, it's time to get over that. Did you know it's the leading cause of war? I'm trying to think of a war that didn't boil down to "I don't like how different you are." The Crusades? "Your religion is different than mine." World War II? Jews. Sure, you can bring up something like the American Revolutionary War and say it was about taxation without representation, but look at it from the British's perspective. Why not grant the colonists the same representation? Because they're dirty colonists halfway around the world, and we're the noble Brits, that's why. They don't deserve that sort of representation. It was "us" versus "them." That's literally what a war is.

Does it stem from institutionalization? That too. The average American hasn't met an Iranian, but right now we're supposed to hate them because we're told of how different they are and how those differences collide with our freedom. And nukes, that one never gets old. Let me tell you, I know a couple of Iranians, and the ones I hate I do so because they're assholes, not because of all that tacky Armani shit they're always wearing or how they treat shirt buttons as prudish suggestions. And that's the way it should be. Judge a person by who they are as a person.

It's tough to break the cycle of using stereotypes to guide your decision-making process, but try. Or at least recognize that maybe you've never met an Italian you've liked because the only Italians you've met were a group of 3rd-generation Italian-Americans in a South Beach nightclub called Smegma. If your Puerto Rican coke dealer has no class and acts like an animal, it's not because he's Puerto Rican, it's because he's a coke dealer. And you're an addict, get some help.

CHAPTER 11

Create Your Own Cheat Codes.

"Up, Up, Down, Down, Left, Right, Left, Right, B, A"
—Konami

Here we go with the fucking arm-chair shrink shit again. There's a psychological finding called the *Benjamin Franklin effect* which states that someone who has done you a favor is more likely to perform another favor for you than they would if they had received a favor from you instead. It sounds counter-intuitive, but Ben Franklin knew his shit. For fuck's sake, he's on the American $100 bill without having been a president. Yeah, Hamilton wasn't a president either, but the dude basically founded the U.S. treasury, and even then he only gets the $10 bill.

Anyway, Benny Boy discovered this when politicking his ass off in Pennsylvania. There was a rival legislator who didn't like him very much. That guy's name doesn't matter, because he didn't tie a key to a kite and let it strike lightning, so let's call him Asshole. In order to change Asshole's perception of him, he wrote Asshole a letter asking him for a favor: allowing Benny to borrow a rare book Asshole has in his collection. Asshole lent him the book, presumably to maintain civility between legislators, and Benny returned it a week later with another note strongly expressing his gratitude. The next time they convened in the House, Asshole spoke to Benny, which he had never done before, and they became great friends for life.

That technique is similar to the *foot-in-the-door* maneuver, where a person gets someone to agree to a large request by first having them agree to a small request. There's also a reverse to that, called the *door-in-the-face technique*, which is making an intentionally preposterous request so that your intended request, which is decidedly less ridiculous, is something they're much more comfortable performing. You fall for that shit all the time. Every time you see an item for sale with a list price scratched out and a sale price, you're being presented with the door-in-the-face method.

So what's your cheat code? You're reading this book because you're an idiot, so you probably know very few, if any. I'll get you started with some.

- When parking in a large parking lot, pull out your smartphone and take a photo of the nearest parking sign. Also, work on your memory, because remembering the two or three alphanumeric characters on the sign shouldn't be that much of a challenge.
- If you try using a credit card and the magnetic strip fails for any reason, put the card in a thin plastic grocery bag and swipe it again. Or, for a better fix, apply a piece of transparent tape over the strip. Or for an even more effective remedy, get a new fucking card.
- If you forget someone's name, ask them for their name. If they look annoyed when they tell you, say, "I meant your last name." You got their name and made them look like the asshole instead.
- Have you tried turning whatever isn't working off and

back on? That should be the first thing you try, unless it's your grandfather's pacemaker you're troubleshooting.

- Here's one for the gentlemen: If you're going on a first date, don't tell your date where you're going or how to dress; simply tell your date to dress however they'd dress for a first date with a guy they really want to see. Have a plan for three different types of venues. Plan for something fun and active, something sexy and romantic, and something casual. When you pick her up (or him; all love is cool, man), let her wardrobe dictate your date. Is she dressed sexy, borderline scandalous? Go to a nice lounge, upscale restaurant, etc. Is she wearing jeans and comfortable shoes? Go bowling or some similar shit you won't obliterate her too badly at when your competitive side comes out. Is she wearing something in between? Try a nice bar. Just avoid the movie theater like the plague. The point of a first date is to get to know each other, and that won't be happening if you're getting to know Johnny Depp's character in the latest Tim Burton movie, which happens to be exactly the same as the last five.

Lastly, use the Internet to find cheat codes. I totally did, and you paid me for it.

CHAPTER 12

Don't Cheat.

*"I would prefer even to fail with honor
than win by cheating."*
—Sophocles

All right you little fucker, before you go start calling me a hypocrite, understand that the previous chapter used "cheat codes" metaphorically. You're not actually cheating the universe, just streamlining the way you do things. If you cheat at Scrabble, you're not streamlining the way you whoop someone's ass, you're fucking cheating.

People hate cheaters. I mean, they really, really hate them. A few years ago, Lance Armstrong was the most popular Armstrong who ever lived. Keep in mind there was another Armstrong who walked on the goddamn Moon for the first time in history. Even so, Lance was the shit. Then it was discovered that he cheated his way through all those Tour de France medals. Now the world hates him so much they're rooting for cancer instead.

There are three fundamental types of cheating: cheating on people, cheating academically, and cheating in games and sports.

Cheating on people can fuck them up pretty badly; the damage that can be done to a person's psyche is brutal. I cheated on my girlfriend once, in her dream, and she was sad for hours. I can only begin to speculate the name of the river she'd throw my severed genitals into if I were unfaithful in reality. It messes with your trust in future relationships, and it puts thoughts you'd rather not have in your mind about the nature of monogamy and how easy it is to cheat.

Academically, cheating primarily hurts yourself but can have an impact on others. I had an engineering professor who stressed, "If you cheat in my class, someone could die." The rationale was that as an engineer, not properly understanding the concepts taught could result in negligence extreme enough to get people killed. I'd personally avoid any bridge designed by anyone belonging to any fraternity that butt-chugged their liquor. (Let me save you an Internet search. Butt-chugging is the act of chugging liquor through your asshole. The goal is to get drunk quicker, for less money, and do the sorts of gay shit typical fraternities love to do while simultaneously being homophobic.) Anyway, cheating in school may get you a passing grade, but for fuck's sake you're supposed to be there to learn. And what the hell is wrong with learning? You lazy bastard.

The last kind, cheating at games and sports, is a murkier topic. Cheating at a board game probably won't do much more than establish a nickname and reputation. You'll be that guy not allowed anywhere near the bank while playing Monopoly, and at worst no one will want to play anything with you, ever. Sure, it's not at the level of betraying someone or building a bridge out of balsa wood, but you're still that guy who cheats. At sports, however, you enter full-fledged assholitude.

In professional sports, the guy is paid for his natural and cultivated athletic ability. The idea is this person is among the best in the world at what they do, be it throwing a ball through a hoop, tackling a guy to the ground, or whatever the fuck goes on in cricket. Kids everywhere look up to athletes. Whether they like it or not, they're role models. So when an athlete cheats, it sends a message to kids that it's cool to take shortcuts or get a reward through dishonest means. (It basically sets them on a path to politics.) And since kids are stupid little shits, they soak that in. Ever notice how kids tend to imitate all the bad things? If you say "motherfucker" and a kid hears it, he's going to drive you mad repeating that word. If you said "microcosm"? Not a fucking peep.

Cheating boils down to dishonesty. People feel betrayed when they believed in you or your abilities only to find out later you're just a goddamn charlatan. Trust is one of those important things you're given very few opportunities to repair, so be wise about it.

Damn it, Lance, how could you? Oh, now I remember, it's because cycling as a sport is just one big-ass cheat-fest.

CHAPTER 13

Limit Your Lying.

"Richard Nixon is a no-good, lying bastard."
—President Harry S. Truman

Getting caught in a lie is a gut-wrenching feeling most of us have experienced. The easiest way to fix that is by not telling any lies. Ever. That's unrealistic and stupid in its own right. Limiting the amount of lying you do is where the sweet spot is.

Whenever people say they never lie, it's a hilariously ironic lie. Everybody lies. There's really nothing wrong with lying provided you keep it to a minimum, keep your lies small, and try not to hurt people. Telling a somewhat unattractive female, "Not gonna lie, you look very pre-op," isn't one of those acceptable lies I'm talking about. I heard a guy say that to a girl's face once after she turned him down. I wasn't sure whether I should've pretended I didn't hear it or been impressed with his creativity.

"White lies," as they're referred to, are the kind where you lie to spare someone's feelings. Those are always OK. Using a clichéd example, if my girlfriend tried on a pair of shorts and asked me if they made her look fat, it would take an executive order from the not-yet-created office of the President of Outer Space for me to say yes. I'm not gonna fall for that shit. Those lies are harmless, and taking a strong anti-lie approach to life would mean having benign little things like that escalate to catastrophic proportions.

"Black lies," as no one refers to them, are the kind where you do it for personal gain. Fraud is a black lie. Cheating is a black lie. Milli Vanilli was a black lie. Black lies actively deceive and hurt others, and getting caught telling a black lie has pretty far-reaching repercussions. Ideally, you shouldn't do these at all.

"Grey lies," another term I just made up, are somewhere in the middle. Pathological liars tend to teeter around this area. I went to high school with a guy who seemed to enjoy lying for the sake of lying. He would make up the most unbelievable horseshit, and even when it became apparent that no one believed him, he pressed on. Don't be that person. You're not getting away with that shit, and years later when you think back to it, you'll realize just how transparent you were. It's cringeworthy, really. As I write this I'm remembering some of the bullshit I told in middle school and how everyone knew. Oh man.

Fuck it, I'll tell you one. In middle school, my best friend and I had Adam Sandler's weird comedy album *What the Hell Happened to Me?* and listened to it constantly. When I say constantly, I mean I could recite the whole thing from beginning to end. In class one day, I was bored and decided to write it. By "write it," of course, I mean I wrote the whole damn thing down on paper. Every word. From his stupid skit about joining a cult to the last stupid song he had on there. One of the cool kids in class (not the jerk kind, just a generally cool kid) sees what I'm writing when I'm about halfway done, and he reads some of it without me noticing. He asked me what I was writing, and being a fucking moron, I said, "I'm writing a script." I don't know why I said that. He seemed excited about that and asked if he could see it and show others. Before I could kindly tell him to go fuck himself (at least in my head—I was painfully shy), he was already reading it out loud. The teacher wasn't in the classroom at the time. Stay with me here. Anyway, people laughed as he deadpanned Adam Sandler's stupid, out-of-context jokes. When he told them all it was my script, people really got into it. I kept getting asked questions, and I answered them with on-the-spot garbage. The crowd, as it were, was excited and chatty about it with me. At the time, I thought people were buying it.

Years later, I'm in college talking to a girl who was in that classroom at the time. I won't forget what she said. Her words were, "You're that kid who lied about writing Adam Sandler's songs, right?"

I cringe every time.

Learn from me, damn it, so my experience be not in vain!

CHAPTER 14

Be Dependable.

"Read my lips, no new taxes."
—Vice President George H.W. Bush

I used to make fun of the douche who would say he has to check his calendar when you ask what he's doing on a certain day. I thought, "Who the fuck writes shit on calendars?" Smart people do. I've learned that wearing glasses makes you smart, listening to NPR makes you smart, and writing shit on calendars makes you smart. People who record future events (not work-related) seem to be more organized than those who don't. And by "seem to be," I mean they're absolutely more organized.

There's nothing wonderful about a person you can't count on. Everyone's got that friend who's never on time; you've begun resorting to tricks like telling them to meet you for dinner two hours earlier than usual. That friend is a scumbag. The thought process that goes into ignoring travel time entirely is astounding. They know they need to be somewhere at 7:00 p.m., it's 6:35 p.m., it takes them twenty-five minutes to get there, and they just ignore it. I would love to science the hell out of their heads to understand which neurons sparked the decision to pin a few more shitty homemade tea cozies on Pinterest for the next fifteen minutes before finally departing.

But you can't just start showing up early to shit either. That's unpleasant as fuck.

Try to remember the old phrase, "The early bird gets the worm." The worm dies in this little story for being up too soon.

You need to be that bird, not the shitty worm, otherwise you'll just get eaten. I mean, yeah, the worm was early too, but he was too early. Don't be overly premature, either. That's probably worse, and you'll end up paying for it.

Imagine you have friends, and those friends are throwing a birthday party. The organizer tells you the party starts at 9:00 p.m. and you show up at 7:30 p.m. Shit isn't going to be ready, so when you show up your friend will be like, "Oh man, I'm glad you're here. Help me set all this shit up." That's what you get for arriving there much too soon. To frame it another way, if you told your friend to come to your house at 8:00 p.m. and they show up at 6:00 p.m., now you've gotta stop whatever the hell you were doing and start getting ready, because you can't just have your friend sitting there while you proceed with business as usual. Only about twenty-seven percent of what I do when I'm home alone involves having underwear on my person, and I imagine it's the same for everyone.

Other times showing up on time isn't about that sort of specific punctuality, but more along the lines of performing the task you agreed to. You may have been baked when you agreed to build your own space program with your best friend, but now that it's time to pay the piper you better either nut the fuck up and get some low-paid immigrant workers into orbit, or explain to your friend what a terrible and possibly illegal idea that is.

When you need to be somewhere, be there. If you need to do something, remember it. Take to the habit of being the douche who writes shit on his calendar.

CHAPTER 15

Avoid Anti-Intellectualism.

"Anti-intellectualism has been
a constant thread winding its way
through our political and cultural life,
nurtured by the false notion
that democracy means that
'my ignorance is just as good as your knowledge.'"
—Isaac Asimov

It has never been fashionable to be a nerd, but there have been many times where the truly brilliant were revered. Then again, Galileo was condemned to house arrest for being the Renaissanciest of Renaissance men, and Socrates was executed for having balls of steel and setting the stage for Western philosophy.

Nowadays you can't really do much without taking advantage of something that someone much smarter than you invented. It's very easy to claim your mobile phone works via magic, or that your car runs on unleaded demon sorcery, or the mere fact that there are currently humans in motherfucking space is a testament to the power of witchcraft. But these things are all brought to you by groups of people vastly smarter than you and me. And let me tell you, I love not having polio, it's amazing that I can press little alphanumeric squares and receive money, and I still can't believe that over forty years ago we strapped a couple of extremophiles to a hunk of metal filled with thousands of tons of liquid propellant and somehow got them to the Moon. My dick still gets hard when I think about an astronaut planting a flag on a space rock, and it's astounding that others forget we've done it six times.

Yet you still find people whose Facebook interests contain the words "Books are for faggots" and "I don't read LOL." Fox News, America's most trusted, unbiased, and fair source of absolute horseshit, established an entire anti-intellectualism branch it calls "the entire program schedule." They tell idiots that the educated elite believe they're better, and that their goal is to keep the idiots down. Being idiots, they believe it. They ignore the fact that the people telling them this are usually educated elites, or if they're not traditionally-educated, they're at least savvy enough to become millionaires with their own fucking television programs.

What needs to be remembered is that the majority of people aren't very intelligent. At the same time, the majority aren't stupid. Most people fall somewhere in the middle, where we make dumb decisions, contribute absolutely zero scientific advancements if transported back in time, and have some trouble helping our kids with their math homework when letters start supplanting numbers. That's average intelligence, and there's nothing wrong with that. But it's important to recognize that those who do fall above that range may know certain things we don't. That's not to say you should take their word as gospel, it just means you need not immediately dismiss them and fear their superior intellect. Otherwise, if you relied on the aptitude of the average person, Apple would be charging $500 for their latest device—a long-ass string between two cups—and people would be buying them. Revolutionary.

Wanna know where you stand? Take an IQ test. Not one of those silly ones you find in quiz sites. If the link to the test is preceded by a link to a test titled, "How long will you survive the zombie apocalypse?" you're in the wrong fucking place. I'm talking a serious, legitimate Stanford-Binet exam. You don't have to broadcast your score or anything; this is purely a personal endeavor. IQ tests aren't perfect by any means, but they're a decent gauge. You will likely land squarely in the average zone, along with most people you know. Congratulations.

Build up your knowledge. Read more books. You may not like novels, and that's fine; there's plenty more to read. It's surprisingly fun to surf Wikipedia for hours, going from link to link. And explaining to people how you started off learning about magma and ended up awwing at Hitler's baby photo never gets old, trust me.

CHAPTER 16

Don't Stick to Misconceptions.

"If we evolved from monkeys,
then why are there still monkeys around?"
—Some fucking idiot

There's this moment we've all experienced. You're in a heated debate with someone over whether or not a duck's quack has an echo. Years ago you were told it doesn't, and because you have the mental faculties of a sleeping hamster, you believed it and are now fervently defending that position. While arguing your case, it hits you. "Holy shit, I'm wrong." Even so, you continue the debate, but now that you know you're wrong, you change tactics. Instead of proving your point, you try to win via logical fallacies, like questioning your opponent's credibility. "What the fuck do you know about duck quacks? You think Chinese buffets are a Chinese conspiracy to make us fat so we'll be easier to invade!"

This is what idiots and politicians do. Rather than admitting you're wrong, you attack your opponent with subject matter irrelevant to the discussion at hand.

Let's say I come up with an amazing weight-loss diet plan. I start telling everyone about it, and it gains traction to the point where its popularity is unprecedented. It's a great diet, you know it's a great diet, everyone knows it's a great diet. But then one day you find out that I like to fuck goats. My goat lust has absolutely nothing to do with the unparalleled efficacy of the diet I invented, but you're a competing dietician and hate my success. So you tell people all about how I seduce goats, play with their

because it concurrently tells physics, chemistry, and biology to go fuck themselves. I've joked about how smartphones work via magic and pleasant dreams, but homeopathy quite literally relies on magic to work. Potions brewed by cartoon witches are more effective than homeopathy, because at least they have more ingredients than just water. Still, homeopathic remedies fly off the shelves, indubitably using magic to do so. The medical community considers homeopathy to be absolute quackery, and has tested various homeopathic remedies countless times and found them demonstrably ineffective.

Most people don't seem to give a shit, though, which is what leads to a low dose of dubiousness among the general populace.

Have you ever received email from a Nigerian claiming he needs help moving his inheritance outside of the country, and he's reaching out to you, a random person thousands of miles away with no apparent international finance acumen, for aid? Most of you have, and most of you don't fall for that. You read that email thinking, "What does this guy think I am, some kind of idiot?" That's the same thing people with healthy skepticism think when they hear about shit like homeopathy. Meanwhile, they're watching rubes count their homeopathic dosages carefully, lest they overdose on fucking tap water.

These days you're considered a buzzkill if you point out when something sounds wrong. That's that anti-intellectualism I discussed earlier. But what do we expect when we indoctrinate our kids with it early on? Santa Claus, the Tooth Fairy, the Easter Bunny. These are all motherfuckers we tell our kids are real, they believe it, and then we pull the rug out from under them and say,

"Surprise, little shits, we made all these guys up!" If it stopped there, our kids would end up more skeptical, which would be a good thing. However, when they ask, "What about Jesus, is he real?" we go apeshit and demand they never question his existence again. No wonder we grow up treating critical thought as that thing we do only when contemplating whether or not to shit at work or wait until we get home.

Every time someone makes a claim which seems even the least bit implausible, question it internally. "Did this guy truly impregnate that stripper and coerce her into having an abortion using her own stripper money, or is he just doing a deplorable job at bragging?"

With that said, don't turn into one of those conspiracy theory nuts. That's unhealthy skepticism. If you find yourself questioning whether or not we landed on the Moon, or whether the 9/11 attacks were an inside job, or thinking that the low-hanging baggy pants style was invented by cops specifically to make it harder for gang members to flee, you're suffering from a case of runaway suspicion. The cure for that is homeopathic—which means there is no cure.

Critical thinking has to start at the micro level with the individual; otherwise, we'll spend the rest of our lives paying $80 for HDMI cables.

CHAPTER 18

Stop Repeating Things You Don't Get.

"I heard on the news that..."
—Some fucking idiot

So, you heard something on the news you feel is important and want to tell others about it. That's cool, information needs to be spread. What's the news?

"I HEARD ON THE NEWS THAT VACCINES CAUSE AUTISM."

Whoa, let me stop you right there. First, no they don't. Second, Jenny McCarthy doesn't know what the fuck she's talking about, nor does she have an advanced degree in anything remotely related to immunology.

This is an example of a crazy lady repeating something she doesn't understand. I don't know exactly where she got the idea from, but If I had to take a wild guess I'd say she noticed her son (who allegedly "had" autism, though experts say his symptoms more closely matched that of Landau–Kleffner syndrome, commonly misdiagnosed as autism) had vaccines administered to him, and in her crazy-ass head she connected the dots using tenuous rationale so sketchy not even lab monkeys stoop that low. It's the same logical leap as saying, "Fuck, I'm HIV positive. It must've been caused by not giving that homeless man change twelve years ago." Then this zany woman goes on talk shows telling every parent with an autistic kid to give them chelation therapy, a process that can result in heart attack, stroke, or cardiac arrest. A process (in that context—it's useful for metal poisoning) which the medical community considers, in medical parlance, "horseshit."

I sympathize with her and what her kid has to go through, I do, but anyone attempting to subvert the benefits of herd immunity needs to promptly shut the fuck up so my future kid doesn't get polio. How is my future son going to support my future cocaine habit by making millions as an NBA superstar if he's got those crippled polio legs?

Most will agree that willful ignorance is a vice. But what many seem to have a problem with is regular ignorance. Like, I don't know some shit I never claimed to know and suddenly I'm the asshole? There's a certain bad connotation tied to the word "ignorance," as though it meant "stupid." Not at all. Ignorance just means you aren't knowledgable about that one particular thing, which every human in existence is guilty of since we haven't invented hoverboards yet. I'm ignorant when it comes to the rearing of baby pandas. If I were handed a baby panda right now, it would be dead in forty-seven minutes flat. I have no idea what to do with a baby panda. If some idiot had told me, "Bro, all you have to do to take care of a baby panda is speak to it in Chinese and feed it baby formula," I would find that a little odd, but with me not knowing any better, the cops would show up to my house because of a noise complaint from my neighbors and get an eyefull of the weirdest scene ever: a bunch of Chinese language books, opened baby formula cans everywhere, and a spazzed-out dude yelling a list of Chinese verbs at a furry little corpse.

Sometimes it's the little crap that gets spread around, those minuscule tidbits which make absolutely no sense that people propagate. Think about the last time you were on Facebook and saw a status update about some little girl who desperately needs an operation, and that she'll receive that operation if the status gets 20,000 "likes." What the fuck, man? Do those people seriously think there's some doctor hovering over Facebook thinking to himself, "Come on, people, just 3,751 more likes until I can save this little girl's life." Why in the everliving fuck would that be a real scenario? Do doctors get paid in "likes" now? Is that what Obamacare was all about? I didn't read the whole thing, so I don't know, and I'm not going to pretend to know.

If you don't know something, don't just bark out some shit to make noise and seem knowledgeable. It makes disseminating factual data that much more difficult. Misinformation is like a virus that spreads by infecting idiots. And I can't stress this enough: Vaccines do not cause autism. Vaccinate your kids, people. Have you ever seen pre-vaccination infant mortality rates? Of course not, because Jenny McCarthy never brought it up on Oprah.

CHAPTER 19

Stop Playing the Blame Game.

"A man can fail many times, but he isn't a failure until he begins to blame somebody else."
—John Burroughs

OK, fine, this chapter's title is a bit misleading. Sometimes blaming is completely warranted. If you were to ask me who started WWI, I'm going to blame Germany. If you ask me about WWII? Germany. If I'm alive for WWIII, you guessed it, Germany. (I mean, at this point it's tradition.) This is about blaming someone else when you've fucked up, or blaming something you don't understand because you need a scapegoat.

These days, every time a kid does something violent, video games, rap, or movies are blamed. It's always video games, rap, or movies. The news goes ahead and presents the stories as a question, then specifically frames that question in order to tell you what to think. "Do video games bring out an insatiable hunger for murder in our youth? More at 11." How the fuck can you ask a question in that way and expect some form of unbiased discourse? How about saying, "Tonight, we'll investigate the pathology of violence in our youth." Same damn message, without putting an idea in people's heads. The worst part is that the media will blame video games, movies, and rap music for warping the minds of our children, then they'll cut to a story about a guy who shot his wife in the face, complete with gory details, mug shots, police reports, dramatic reenactments, and interviewing morons about whether or not they feel safe (spoiler alert: they don't).

As of 2012, the United States has a bigger military budget than the next fourteen highest-budget nations combined (a total of forty-one percent of the global military budget) and we've been at war for over a decade. Yet people have the balls to blame video games for violent behavior? Yeah, I'm sure Jack the Ripper played tons of Grand Theft Auto before going out and killing whores, and Stalin was widely regarded as a Call of Duty aficionado.

The blame game is closely-related to the excuse game. It can start with either one, then lead to the other. The media is quick to blame video games for violent behavior; we already know that. Let's say a hypothetical study were done on the subject, and scientists concluded that video games were, in fact, *not* the cause of increased violence. That would mark the end of the blame game and cue the first inning of the excuse game. "We have to run those news reports because it's the only way to attract viewers!" they'd say. Home run, Fox News! (Fun fact, a Fox News clip was the first and only time in my life I've witnessed someone commit suicide, and it was a guy shooting himself in the head.) But they're totally right, Jeffrey Dahmer learned to eat people through nightly Pac-Man sessions.

Before you start passing blame around, make a little introspective journey real quick to make sure you're not just looking for a way to divvy out responsibility. I was late to work yesterday, and I could easily criticize the elevators in my condo for taking too long, or I could just man up and admit that I wasted time sitting on the edge of my bed for eight minutes trying to come up with the name of a relative I could kill off so my boss would let me grieve on my cloud-like bed for a while.

This is one of the shortest chapters in the book, and I blame it on the next one.

CHAPTER 20

Stop Making Bullshit Excuses.

"Excuses are like assholes, Taylor,
everybody got one."
—Sgt. O'Neill, *Platoon*

If I had a nickel for every time someone let me down and gave me a bullshit excuse, I'd throw nickel a them. It's frustrating as hell when you agree on something, whatever it may be, only to have your plans ruined by an asshole who can't keep his word. The worst is when you fall for the hook and look like a moron when you inevitably discover it was a ruse. "Oh, they have WMDs? Then yeah, dude, we totally have to go in there and liberate. Let's liberate the fuck out of them."

People are afraid of turning others down, unless they're sociopaths. If you ask a friend to help you move and they don't want to do it, you'll get a response like, "I'd love to, but I'll have to see if I can, because…" followed by a stream of lies. You know they simply don't want to. They know you know they don't want to. Wouldn't it be so much easier to say, "Sorry, I don't want to do that because I honestly prefer masturbating to the sounds of fat people on an elliptical than to move shit for somebody else"? But we're not allowed to do that, because of social customs. It's like Persians and "t'aarof." You're probably not familiar with t'aarof since there's an embargo and all, so allow me to explain. In the simplest way I can describe it, t'aarof is a Persian custom wherein someone offers you something; you're supposed to decline it. They keep insisting you take it, but you have to decline. This goes on and on until someone relents. If you go into some Persian guy's house and he says, "Please, my friend, have sex with my beautiful daughter," you're supposed to say no, then he'll implore you to do it and provide you with a handful of condoms. If you say yes, you're a complete asshole, but to save face the guy has to let you fuck his daughter, and then he'll hate you forever even though he offered it in the first place.

But back to excuses. Inventing alibis is akin to crying wolf; the more you do it, the more likely others are to dismiss your cover story as yet another set of fibs, and they'll judge you in the future. Part of your newfound non-idiocy is being upfront with people.

Pretend for a moment your buddy asked you to go help him buy some furniture at IKEA. Obviously, you don't want to go there. No one wants to go there. IKEA is never a couple of blocks away; it's always too fucking far away, because they require the right property. I think IKEA needs to be facing Sweden the same way Muslims have to pray facing Mecca. Anyway, you come up with some reason why you can't. "I, uh, have a date that day. With a hot, um, Lithuanian girl I met at, uh, the ice store." Your cop-out was stupid. I mean, really, the ice store? Your friend brushed it off, but now, in case he brings that shit up again, you gotta make up a story, so you go on Wikipedia and kill a few hours learning everything you can about Lithuania. Next time you see him, he asks you about that Lithuanian girl, and you're like, "What? Oh, yeah, that girl. It was cool, she's into falconry and shit. She told me she was an illegal dogfight referee back in Vilnius, the capital of Lithuania.

Speaking of Lithuania, did you know that the service sector encompasses the largest share of their GDP?" Plus you need to remember all that shit in case he brings it up a few months later when you're at a bar and some lanky-ass Lithuanian basketball player gets shown on TV. Don't do it, just tell him the truth. "I hate IKEA. Fuck IKEA." He's a man. He can go to IKEA without holding your fucking hand.

Avoiding the excuse game makes you a more honest person. I'm not saying you should never lie; that would be catastrophic. Just, you know, be upfront.

CHAPTER 21

Bring Value to the World.

"A man who dares to waste one hour of time has not discovered the value of life."
—Charles Darwin

Human beings, as a species, are selfish creatures. Our entire lives boil down to wanting things. We want delicious food, we want a big house, we want a nice car, we want to be sexually satisfied: we want all sorts of shit. There's nothing wrong with that, and not everyone's intent is motivated purely by self-interest. A parent may want a big house to give all of their kids enough room, whereas a rapper may want a big house to show off how wealthy he is. But how do you get those things?

Well, think about how you get things you want. You go to an ice cream parlor (you fat fuck, you) and say, "Give me that chocolate brownie mix chocolate ice cream thing with chocolate sprinkles and chocolate fudge and chocolate chocolate, chocolate chocOLATE CHOCOLATE!!" They give you the ice cream, and you give them money. To get something, you give something. How did you earn that money? You sat in an office all day posting shit on Facebook and occasionally performing a task someone finds value in; in return, they give you money. That money came from someone who found value in what your company as a whole does. They got that money from their company, which found value in them and which, in turn, provided a valuable service to another person, who also did something a company wanted. To quote a brilliant man quoting an idiot, "It's turtles all the way down." This, whether you like it or not, is the way the world, nay, the universe works. Our environment needs our planet to survive, our planet needs our sun to survive, our sun needs hydrogen to survive—turtles, turtles, turtles.

Beyond your shitty job, what value do you bring to the world? I'm not talking about shit you are, like, "I'm kind" or "I'm smart," I'm referring to what you do. No one cares if you're nice or knowledgeable unless you do something with it, like build a time machine while being really, really polite to people as you do it. Actions are what matter. In 2011, when Poseidon assholishly destroyed northeast Japan with salt water, it wasn't the prayers from all the sad white people in the West that rebuilt the Japanese infrastructure in, like, fifteen minutes. It was all those Japanese motherfuckers toiling day and night to make sure they got electricity back up, in order to power all those little gadgets and robots they love to make. If recovering from storm damage were all down to prayers, Haiti would've moved forward so quickly they'd be planting a Haitian flag on the Moon right next to an American one. (And then, of course, the United States would send another Moon mission to move that American flag to a nicer part of the Moon. Americans take "white flight" seriously.)

Tell me something you do of value. Pretend I'm that guy or girl you've got a crush on and you're trying to impress me. What could you tell me that you do, so I'll let you fornicate me? Like I said, humans are selfish by necessity, so if you want someone in your life you need to give them a reason to invest in you as a person. Saying "I'm nice" is worthless unless it comes attached to something like, "I volunteer at the children's hospital and dress up as Batman for all the little kids." Being nice doesn't mean you'll finish last; the problem is that self-proclaimed nice guys have little else to offer, whereas the tattooed, motorcycle-riding bad boys that take the girls away from the nice guys can at least offer a motorcycle ride and some short-lived excitement, which is presented right there, at face value. There's an inherent worth in that. Instead of describing yourself as a nice guy, describe yourself as an artist, or a poet, or whatever the hell it is you can actually do, no matter how borderline-homosexual it may make you sound.

That's not to say that the more money you have, the better you are. Paris Hilton has more money than Albert Einstein ever had, but who would you call a bigger success? Thousands of years from now, humans will still talk about Einstein the way we talk about Plato, but you'll be hard-pressed to find any mention of Paris Hilton, just like nowadays you don't hear of any Roman senator's talentless, whorish daughter who liked to party like it's MCMXCIX. When I talk about providing value, I don't mean you have to be a millionaire, I mean you need to do something of benefit to others. Paris Hilton may be talentless and entitled, but I'll begrudgingly admit she at least brings something to the table in the form of entertainment, so she's doing her part. Are you?

Find out where your value lies, then offer it to the world to see what you get back. It could end up being something you wanted. Or it could just be ice cream, which is pretty cool too, unless you're diabetic.

CHAPTER 22

Procrastinate Less.

> *"I'll do it later."*
> —Some fucking idiot

I'll write this chapter later.

CHAPTER 23

Don't Be Afraid to Change.

*"Everyone thinks of changing the world,
but no one thinks of changing himself."*
—Leo Tolstoy

Change can be either good or bad. Like, if you had a sex-change operation, that change would be good if you wanted it, and bad if you didn't. There are those who hate change. It doesn't really matter what's changing. Their routine is being disrupted, and their inability to adapt makes them uneasy. This is a very dumb way to live, because your routine may very well suck.

Before my girlfriend moved in with me, I was a typical bachelor. How bachelor? Here are some examples:

The mop I owned was in its original packaging.

I could only sleep on one side of the bed, because on the other side was a pile of clothes, unless I expected company, in which case the clothes ended up back in the dryer.

Oh, and also toilet-rim pubes.

You get the idea. Anyway, once she moved in, she started changing my habits little by little. Now I drink tea daily, from a tea cup, on a tea cup plate, with a biscuit, while my legs are crossed (the European way, not the cowboy way). That's fucking amazing! I ate like a fat fucking slob before and should've weighed 400 pounds. The only reason I didn't is because I've got the metabolism of a Jamaican sprinter. Anyway, now she cooks healthier meals and I'm going to the gym more often. She used to equate sleeping on my shitty bed to sleeping like a homeless person; now we've got that memory foam scientific NASA witchcraft thing and sleep on a cloud.

Those were all changes to my routine, but my routine was that of a fucking moron. Now I'm not as messy, I'm healthier, and I sleep better.

Try to be a little more receptive to change when it presents itself. Or hell, even if it doesn't present itself. Analyze yourself and find your shortcomings. I don't know, maybe you smack your lips like a fucking ungulate when you eat or chew gum. Or perhaps you use the same word or term all the time. "You know what I mean?" You can, and should, change that.

Don't be afraid of changing your opinion, either. Imagine you were a huge football fan back in 1994. Then, one day in June, you heard about O.J. Simpson in a police chase. Being a fan of football, you defended O.J. "Man, it's probably just LAPD chasing a guy because he's black," you said. Later, you learned more details about the story. "There's no way the Juice killed anybody, man, that glove doesn't even fit." If today you still thought O.J. didn't kill those people, that would be one of those examples where changing is cool. You keep receiving more and more facts, but your stubborn ass refuses to evolve your views.

Even if it's not a change you're welcoming, you should still embrace it. You don't need to be like, "Fuck yes, bankruptcy!" but maybe don't treat it like it's the end of the world. Instead, try to view it more positively, like, "Well, at least I don't owe anyone money anymore." It may sound stupid, but keeping a positive outlook works. Even if you're just fooling yourself, people are a lot more productive when they're happy. That's why smart companies strive to increase employee morale. Google has fucking slides in their headquarters. Yeah, slides, like the ones at playgrounds.

Pick something you don't like about yourself and change it. Just make sure it doesn't hurt anyone, obviously. Can't have people thinking, "I don't like that I'm not a serial killer."

CHAPTER 24

Shake Things Up the Right Way.

*"Those who cannot change their minds
cannot change anything."*
—George Bernard Shaw

Back in high school, I had a history teacher who played the bagpipes in class during our silent reading period. I'm unsure of whether or not silent reading periods were the norm elsewhere, but in my school we had about thirty minutes at the beginning of each day where we were supposed to read something—anything. Mr. Pinks was my teacher's name, and if I had to guess, I would say he had read somewhere that music helped with learning and data retention. Being the hands-on sort of educator he was, the decision to play an instrument used to march soldiers into war and souls into the afterlife came naturally to him. I mean, it makes sense, right? Who wouldn't love to read over what sounds like a pregnant cat being tortured for the location of a fugitive terrorist leader? If he left his bagpipes at home, he played the fiddle. The fucking fiddle. I'd rather listen to a pair of blown airplane-bought headphones playing Korean pop.

Trying to shake things up is admirable and necessary. Doing it the wrong way at the wrong time makes you look like a moron. It's a matter of having right ideas versus wrong ideas. There's an obesity epidemic in America right now, there's no doubt about that. Shaking things up the right way would mean creating a push for fitness and eating healthier. Instead, KFC decided to introduce the Double Down, which consists of two fried chicken breast fillets sandwiching cheese, bacon, and some sort of sauce where the scent of it alone lowers your life expectancy by a couple of hours. This is the wrong kind of shaking things up.

Step out of your comfort zone every once in a while. Are you afraid of horses because you don't trust anything with mohawks? Fuck it, go horseback riding! The worst thing that could happen is you fall off the horse and die, but that's, like, relatively rare. You can stay afraid of horses for the rest of your life if you really want to, or you can break that cycle by trying something new.

I don't know who said this, but there's a quote about how doing the same thing over and over and expecting different results is the very definition of insanity. Quite literally, that's not the definition of insanity, though in spirit it makes sense. I think it may have been Einstein who said that, or maybe people just attribute it to him because he was a fucking genius, and when a genius thing is said, you think, "It must've been the only genius I know of who said it." That's a terrible way to logic, but whatever, man, let's roll with it.

Shaking things up is a requirement if you believe that definition, and who wouldn't? Even monkeys learn that shit. I guarantee if you go to a zoo right now and throw a plastic banana in the chimp exhibit, the chimp will fall for it. Throw another one, the chimp will fall for it again. The third time he'll be a little more hesitant. By the fourth or fifth time he'll ignore you altogether. By the tenth time, guess what? You're dumber than the fucking chimp. The chimp gave up on that shit long ago, and you're still standing at the edge throwing fake plastic bananas, which you spent money on, looking at your friends and saying, "Haha, that stupid chimp. Watch, he'll go for it again. You'll see." There's something about human stubbornness which outweighs logic and reason. We perform that sort of cognitive bias all the time.

"This time it's going to be different!" That's an idiot's mantra. Instead of blowing air into a sheepskin sac, Mr. Pinks should've just played some Mozart at a low volume. From a CD, and not on his shitty fiddle, either.

CHAPTER 25

Tip Correctly.

"If a guy is skilled at anything, that's attractive.
There's something very primal
about that and, sure,
it can be as simple as figuring out the tip quickly.
It's really cool when a guy tips 20 percent
quickly and effortlessly
so that when the check comes,
he opens it and signs his name and done."
—Danica McKellar

Like Winnie from *The Wonder Years* just, um, eloquently stated in that quote above, figuring out how to properly tip is very useful. Tipping is something Europeans do better than their New World counterparts in that they don't tip at all. But this chapter isn't about how the tipping culture is retarded. We already live in it, so we might as well live in it properly.

I have absolutely no science to back this up, but I firmly believe that people who don't tip well are collectively the Antichrist. Ask any server in a restaurant and they'll concur. If a bad tipper ever wrote a memoir, it would start with, "I've killed one, maybe twelve people in my life." There's just something inherently evil about a person who is fully aware that servers live on their gratuities, yet refuses to contribute.

When done right, a tip should be commensurate with the

quality of service. The tipping baseline is fifteen percent. A decent job, which is at least usually the case, obligates the baseline. Exemplary service of course commands a higher gratuity. Now, if the server was less than stellar, such as calling your mother a whore and wiping his ass on your napkin before rubbing it on your face, you can consider dropping it to ten percent. The only time you should ever decrease it below that threshold is for any sort of unforgivable offense, like genocide, puppy murder, and quoting *Twilight*. Aside from that, just pay the goddamn tip.

With that said, the concept of a "tip jar" is a parallel to getting away with murder.

It seems like everywhere you go these days, there's a comically-sized jug with a piece of paper taped onto it that reads "TIPS." Everyone involved in that operation is paid a normal wage, yet they encourage you to overpay for a job they're already paid to perform. This is a flat-out abuse of the tipping system and fuels the fire for those who hate forced gratuity. Now, it's important to understand that dropping currency in a tip jar is entirely voluntary, but that doesn't take away from the fact that the tip jar's pervasiveness is a misuse of the philosophy. It's not a stretch to imagine people seeing tip jars everywhere and becoming desensitized to leaving a gratuity even where it's warranted.

Think about how weird it would be if you finished your dental appointment and on your way out heard the distinct rattle of loose change. You turn around and see one of the hygienists holding up a bucket with cutesy doodles of smiling teeth and mouthwash bottles. I don't know about you, but after that floss-raping I was just administered I'm not about to give them any more of my money. (No, of course I don't floss every day, who the fuck flosses every day? And, listen asshole, I bled as you flossed me not because my gums are particularly unhealthy but because you flossed my gums with the same fervor as an assassin using chicken wire to choke his victims to death uses. Oh God. So much blood.)

Treat tipping the way you should be treating alcohol. If it's presented to you in a jar, for your own good, you should have nothing to do with that.

CHAPTER 26

Save Your Money.

"What's a soup kitchen?"
—Paris Hilton

Let's imagine you just won the lottery after I dedicated an entire chapter to telling you there's no way you're going to win. No one in the history of ever has responded to the question of what they're going to do with their winnings by saying, "I'm going to save ninety percent of it." Rather than saving most of it, the average person would blow it on hookers, coke, gold-plated objects, charities, or family. Someone with a severely impaired moral compass could knock all those out in one day.

Up until about a year ago, the only money I had saved up were a couple of two-dollar bills and Sacajawea golden dollar coins that I keep in my fart box. Before you declare me insane, I don't actually keep farts in that box; I only call it my fart box because it's something I started as a kid. Think about it. If you label something "FART BOX," what's the likelihood that someone will open it, lest they be bombarded by putrid flatulence that has been stewing in dank humidity for an undeterminable period of time? Right, no one ever opened that shit. It was the best safeguard I could afford. It's the same logical leap employed by people without security systems who keep security company signs on their lawns, except my logic includes farts.

At some point, the reality of life strikes, and you become aware of your own net worth. If you want some discouragement, go online and find a tool to estimate your net worth. For most of you, it'll be the most depressing set of digits you've seen since that girl gave you a fake phone number which turned out to be a rejection hotline. For the rest of you that joke doesn't work because you're women, but you're still broke. This predicament stems from stupidity. If you take home $3,000 per month after taxes, your rent shouldn't be $1,500. Get a roommate or live in a shittier neighborhood. No, you don't need to live in the ghetto and learn to Keanu Reeves the hell out of some bullets; you just need to make sure you're only spending at most a third of your income on housing.

So you took my advice and are now living in an apartment a block away from squalor. However, you're saving an extra $500 every month. You're welcome. The important thing now is to keep your other expenses down. Unless you're one of those people with a juvenile addiction to sneakers you'll probably only wear once, your main expense is food. Settle down, I'm not calling you fat. Just think about it for a second: If you don't pack your lunch for work, you're likely spending anywhere between $8–$20 per day on lunch. Factor in what you eat for dinner and on the weekends, and it starts to add up. Sourcing this is sketchy at best, but I'd wager that the average American adult consumes roughly $250 (a.k.a. "The Somalian Million") worth of groceries each month in an effort to thwart starvation. That's groceries, by the way. If you spend a bunch on lunch food on your workdays, you'll need to add that to your total. There's very little you can do on that front without sacrificing your quality of life, unless you spend what scholars refer to as "a fuckload" on junk food (in which case, lowering your intake will dramatically increase your quality of life). Figure out how much you spend on food each month and try working around that number. Also, try working out, you fat shit. Now I am calling you fat.

As a young adult, entertainment is paramount, which means there's probably a lot being spent there, too. Women have it best in this situation. If you're at least a moderately attractive woman, and most of you are, you shouldn't be spending a dime on a night out. This isn't a case of sexism, it's about taking advantage of those titties. If some moron wants to buy you a drink at a bar, take it. There's no obligation to talk to the guy; alcohol isn't a binding contract. Right now there are millions of starving children in need of aid, millions of refugees, and millions requiring healthcare. If, in the quest of pussy, that guy was enough of an asshole to buy a stranger in a first-world country a cocktail instead of helping out those millions in dire need, then he deserves you taking it and drinking it in protest. It's your duty. On the other hand, guys have it tough. Clubs? Ladies free! Gay clubs? Ladies free! Lesbian clubs? Men highly frowned upon! I'd call us oppressed if we didn't literally control the world.

It all boils down to cutting your costs to the point where you can put away a decent chuck of change. You don't have to change your lifestyle dramatically, just live someplace you can afford and try to ball a little less hard. I promise you, saving up to visit Machu Picchu is a much more life-changing event than spending The Somalian Million on a bottle of vodka in your city's newest lounge full of people who pretend to ball as hard as you.

CHAPTER 27

Take Your Job Seriously.

> *"All labor that uplifts humanity has dignity and importance and should be undertaken with painstaking excellence."*
> —Martin Luther King, Jr.

If you're having job problems, I feel bad for you, son. I got 99 problems but an unfulfilling workplace doesn't happen to be one of them. If you hate your work and end up putting very little effort into it, I take back the pity—you're a dumbass. Not enjoying it is one thing, but half-assing it because you wanted to be a cop instead of a security guard not only annoys the hell out of others, it actively hurts you as well.

On average, we spend eight hours per day at work. Let's (conservatively, might I add) put two hours down for commute and lunch. That's ten work-related hours spent each weekday. Pretend you're a healthy adult who gets at least seven hours of sleep each night. Between exercise, showering, and fucking, you have maybe five hours to do whatever it is you do during your weekdays. During the week, you see your stupid coworkers' faces more than you see your family. You came out of your mother's vagina, and you see her less than you do the random nobody in the cubicle next to you who eats chips way too loudly and pisses you off every time he blows his nose or performs some other inconsequential bodily noise. The point is, you spend a lot of time at work, so why would you put in the bare minimum amount of effort, when putting in more effort means moving up in the company and having a more fulfilling career?

It's not just about moving up, it's also about pride in what you do. There's no shame in being in the unskilled workforce, so don't act like there is. That goes for people who actively look down on those with unskilled jobs, too. If I hear you deride someone for being a janitor or a fast food worker, I'm going to smack you in the mouth. Those people don't make enough money to then be shit on by a bunch of immature assholes who don't understand the value of work. The way you should act at work is the way strippers act whenever anyone gives them money. Sure, you don't have to jiggle your titties at anyone and rub up against a clothed erection, but you should have a big, possibly fake smile on your face.

Your job performance could make or break someone's day. If a person's first encounter with another human happens to be unfavorable, that may set the tone for their day. I've started my morning off by having a woman sell me a doughnut while treating me like an early 20th-century Irish immigrant arriving at Ellis Island. The eye-rolls. The sighing. It was almost as if I was forcing her to do something against her will. It's a fucking doughnut, lady, not a plantation.

Oh, and one more thing. You need to maintain a decent relationship with your coworkers. Try to stay away from friction —of both kinds! The first kind is stuff like getting into arguments or being highly confrontational. It's OK to dislike someone, but butting heads with them will lead you nowhere fast. The second is the kind of friction you get when a penis rubs up against a vagina. Avoid that shit. It bears repeating: DON'T FUCK

YOUR COWORKERS. Some people think it's fine, but it's not fine. It causes more problems than it solves, and there are literally billions of other dicks and pussies in the world, so you don't need to relegate yourself to one on a coworker that is only circumstantially hot. That is, "office hot." Someone who is a ten in the office and only like a six at best, once you clock out.

Office relationships are stupid for many reasons. To give you a couple: What if it doesn't work out? What if the other person is fucking nuts, and now you have to deal with the fallout during the majority of your waking moments throughout the greater part of your week? That strain could make your superiors take notice and take action. And what if it actually does work out? Do you really think it's wise to see your lover all day at work and all night at home? Nobody loves that hard. Shit, I barely even love myself that hard, and my ego is bigger than yours.

Do your fucking job, bro. Spend your time wisely.

CHAPTER 28

Shit At Work.

*"Finding a quote about pooping at work
is nigh impossible."*
—Orlando Winters

One of the most satisfying things (on multiple levels) you can do with your time is shit while at work. Billing your company for a bowel movement ranks up there with "don't get herpes" in the list of things to do before you die.

To put things into perspective, let's say you earn $20 an hour at your job. If you scoffed at that or thought to yourself, "Yeah, right. I make more," you need to revisit the chapter about pretentiousness. Anyway, $20. I'm not going to pretend to know how long it takes you to crap, but I usually clock in at around the fifteen-minute mark. Remember, the art of defecation isn't all about speed, it's about relaxation. And there's nothing more relaxing than excreting a mass of decomposed, compressed waste matter through a hole many agree provides more than just a disposal mechanism. That's why they call them "restrooms." If you're one of those people who is in and out in mere minutes, you're doing it wrong. The only time you should be ejecting anything out of your anus that quickly is if you're running drugs for impatient Colombians or you heard the doorknob jiggle and haven't quite stepped out of the closet yet.

Fifteen minutes: that's the sweet spot. You get ample time for a calculated release and the opportunity to catch up on any multiplayer turn-based games against friends. Feel free to take longer if you have some other things you need to do, like reserving a flight, ordering take-out, or working on a book.

At that time frame, provided you have a bowel movement every day, you're being paid approximately $1,300 annually to pinch a loaf. If you're a salaried employee, calculating this becomes decidedly more esoteric. If your "regular hours" are from 9:00 a.m. to 5:00 p.m., and you manage to poop and leave at 5:00 p.m., then you're earning doo-doo dollars. Anything later than that, and it's covered under the salaried time.

Some people don't like to crap in the workplace, for a multitude of reasons including fecal anxiety or disdain for toilet tissue half a step away from sandpaper, and that's understandable. You're not an idiot for that. But if you have no qualms about doing your business in your place of business, yet you refuse to do it, you're being an idiot. Why the hell would anyone sacrifice their own time when they could spare it at work? Your superiors get paid to shit all over you at work, so the way I see it, you'd only be evening things out.

With that said, if you do decide to partake in this activity, there are a couple of things you need to know.

First, don't brag about it to your coworkers. I know people who have their restroom time metered, as absurd as that sounds, to cut down on their exploiting a biological function. Can you imagine looking at your paycheck and seeing a deduction with the note "DEFECATION TIME"? That's awful. You know who else metered restroom use? The Nazis. No, I don't have any evidence to support that.

Second, try not to make it at exactly the same time each day.

I found this out the hard way. I'm a fairly methodical person, so I kept to a strict schedule. I wasn't being sneaky or anything, but I didn't consider that someone could be logging my restroom use. It turns out the receptionist everyone in my office hates does, maybe out of obligation, but more than likely out of pervasive interest. One day just before I left to take a shit so glorious it pleasured my prostate, she said, "Before you go to the restroom, can you give me the number for the conference call so I can have it set before you get back?" She finished setting it up right as I returned, like fucking clockwork. If my shit hadn't just made me reflexively orgasm just minutes prior, I would've been pissed.

Lastly, don't abuse your power. Thirty-minute shits are pushing it, so try to limit it a bit. If at any point your legs fall asleep, you've gone too far. That's your body telling you to get the fuck up. But it's your prerogative if you dip into your lunch hour for extra time to think of a fifty-point word utilizing the triple-word bonus. That's all on you.

If used properly, work shits could be one of the most efficient uses of your time. And don't let anyone tell you there's something wrong with doing it, either. There's an old saying, "Don't shit where you eat." It says nothing about where you work.

CHAPTER 29

Don't Drive Like An Asshole.

*"Americans will put up with anything
provided it doesn't block traffic."*
—Dan Rather

They say the only certainties in life are death and taxes. I believe there's one more certainty: everyone thinks their city has the worst drivers.

As Americans, we need to shut the fuck up with that mantra immediately. I've driven in the third world before, and even the most desolate, *Mad Max*-esque intersections in Detroit pale in comparison to a little Dominican street corner where the traffic signs are written in the town you're in's local slang—and no one actually obeys them.

Driving like an asshole may be tolerable in places where drinking the water is in itself a recreational drug, but not everywhere else. It doesn't just make you a dickhead, it makes you an idiot.

Due to the fact that paying constant attention to your speedometer is unrealistic and dangerous, most of us speed at one point or another. It happens. On the other hand, if you speed over typical distances because you believe it'll get you to your destination quicker, you're terrible at math. Haven't you noticed how Google always seems to employ some sort of black magic in their mapping feature? It's always correct in its assessment on how long a specific trip will take. Try it. Map a random 10-mile route in your city, look at Google's estimate, and start driving. If it said 18 minutes, you'll get there in 18 minutes. If you exceed the speed limit by 20 mph (anything beyond that is approaching criminal negligence), you'll get there in roughly 18 minutes, minus a few seconds. SECONDS. Because math. On a 10-mile straightaway, if you're traveling 60 mph, you'll hit the end in 10 minutes. If you're traveling 80 mph, you'll do it in 7 minutes, 30 seconds. Two-and-a-half minutes might sound like an amazing amount of time saved to then use up procrastinating on your smartphone, but that's assuming a perfect, no-stop, 10-mile trek. The reality is it won't work like that, since you'll spend a lot of that time in local city traffic. You'll end up saving 30 seconds if all the stars and traffic lights align. But yeah, it's totally important to save those precious seconds at the expense of increased gas consumption and a potential speeding ticket. Those status updates aren't going to write themselves!

But the real culprits are those who take assholery to unprecedented levels.

Blocking an intersection is both dangerous and idiotic. If a firetruck is on its way to save the day, blocking an intersection could cost lives, preferably yours if you're blocking it and the firetruck rams through you on its way to rescue a kitten stuck in a tree. As you sit there, impeding traffic while avoiding any eye contact with the multiple scorned drivers around you piercing your soul with their gazes, you sparked a far-reaching chain reaction of tumultuous traffic. What do you do in that situation?

To answer that question, ask yourself another. Have you ever let someone merge into your lane or go in front of you while you're stopped at a light and they're trying to get out of a parking lot, thus prompting the "thank you" hand wave? That's a sign of a gracious driver. (It's also the sign of a gracious driver who just fucked up traffic for everyone.) That small gesture, if you substitute "thank you" for "I'm sorry," is enough to ease most drivers. If you pull an idiot move, apologizing is the best recourse. Even if you're not really sorry, at least fake it. It'll assuage the resentment felt by everyone around you, and since it's nigh impossible for anyone who isn't a gay stylist to transmit sarcasm in silence from twenty feet away, they'll believe you.

Learn to drive properly and avoid the common mistakes made by idiot drivers. The leftmost lane on the highway is for passing. Use your turn signals. Don't move at the same speed as the people next to you, which blocks the path for everyone behind you. Don't tailgate unless there's a barbecue involved. Don't honk at the person in front of you when they didn't move within 0.003 seconds after the light turned green. Don't lean your seat back so damn far. Don't ride your brakes unless your name is Vin Diesel, and if you are Vin Diesel, stop being Vin Diesel.

Just don't drive like shit, at least not consciously. We spend way too much time on the road to deal with this kind of bullshit. If you happen to fuck up, the least you can do is apologize.

CHAPTER 30

There's No Need to Be Pretentious.

"And the Screen Actors Guild Award goes to…"
—Some actor

Overly pretentious people can eat a bowl of cancer. Although, knowing them, it has to be the rarest of cancers, like synovial sarcoma, because they don't touch those typical pedestrian cancers that celebrities survive all the time.

You're not better than me. I don't know you, but I can tell you right now that you're not better than me. Here's something else I'll tell you. I used to suck my thumb for longer than most kids. Some would say it's because my parents didn't allow me to use pacifiers, and douchebag frat guys would probably say it's because I secretly wanted to suck cock. My parents tried everything to wean me off that behavior, because it's ridiculous and it would have adverse effects on my smile alignment. One time when I was about five or six my mother dipped my thumb into my younger sister's feces-ridden diaper in hopes that it would gross me out and I would never put my thumb in my mouth again. Instead, as an act of defiance, I looked her straight in the eye and slowly stuck my thumb directly in my mouth, fecal matter and all. From that day forward, my parents never questioned my resolve again, though eventually my father got me to stop sucking my thumb by promising me a bike if I did so.

To put it more succinctly, I've literally had shit in my mouth. You're still no better than I am, and conversely I'm no better than you. Pretentious people feel as though they are inherently superior human beings for one reason or another. I told you that story to illustrate to you that no matter who you are, no matter how smart, classy, intelligent, cultured, suave, personable, successful, sophisticated, or noble you may believe yourself to be, you're still subject to human behavior. And human behavior involves a lot of shit you keep private. For example, Elizabeth II, Queen of the United Kingdom and the Commonwealth Realms, farts. She farts, pisses, shits, and on occasion examines her royal stool. She has also no doubt performed all sorts of things in the bedroom. It's not like it was back in the day where you'd have some guy announce, "Bring forth the royal cum buckets!" and they'd bring lots of whores for the king to defile, but to assume the current queen is a prude just because she looks so sweet and grandmotherly on television is naïve. My grandma has told me some dirty shit, so I wouldn't put it past Her Majesty to have told Prince William a couple of things he should do to Kate's "little countess." Once again, no matter who you are, you're still human.

An elevated sense of self-importance is a big chunk of what creates a pretentious douche. If you encounter yourself doing things like defending Apple when they do asshole shit, you're likely snobbier than you're willing to admit. Same goes for subtly providing information of your perceived worth.

Want some advice? Don't tell someone a story by giving them more information than the story necessitates; otherwise, people are going to roll their eyes so hard at you they'll see their own gray matter. "I have a son who's studying law at Harvard, and he said the gas prices in Cambridge are high! Can you believe that?" Why the fuck was that first part important to the story in any way? You could've just said your son lives in Cambridge and he says gas prices are high. If your son studied at ITT Technical Institute or any other CWTC (College With Television Commercials), you wouldn't mention it. You'll never hear someone say, "I have a son who's studying pencil sharpener repair at Collegiate University National Tech School, and he says gas prices in Poughkeepsie are high, and also that he hates his life! Can you believe that?" Mostly because CUNTS doesn't exist, but also because that's sad as hell.

Look, if you want to brag a bit about something you're proud of, fine. What you can't be doing is tearing down others to do so, or masquerading your gloating so it looks as though you've only casually showed off. That sort of behavior serves to alienate people, leaving a shitty taste in their mouths. And take it from me, I know exactly what shit tastes like.

CHAPTER 31

Seriously Though, Procrastinate Less.

"We'll do it live, fuck it!"
—Bill O'Reilly

"I'm smart, but I'm lazy." That's such a cop-out. No one really gives a damn what you're capable of if you're never going to get around to it. When was the last time they gave a Nobel prize to a scientist for "hypothetically" decoding the human genome? That's why every parent in the world knows that when they go to a parent/teacher conference and the teacher says, "He has so much potential," the teacher means, "He's not doing any of the fucking work I assign him. At all."

Potential without ambition is absolutely worthless. That baby your Facebook friend won't stop posting photos of has the potential to be a serial killer, but potential means dick if you don't actually go through with it. So go ahead, little Facebook baby, reach for the stars. And then stab them to death and dance a waltz with the bodies, or whatever the hell your *modus operandi* is.

I've found that the easiest way to overcome procrastination is by disassociating yourself from whatever distracts you. For example, I like Wikipedia surfing. I really, really like it. I've spent back-to-back hours in the office learning about the evolution of armadillos when all I meant to do was take a few seconds to find out whether Haskell is a statically or dynamically typed programming language (it's static; you're welcome). If I wish to get something done, I'll avoid Wikipedia at all costs until my task

124

is complete. Whatever it is you do that stops you from getting work done, cut that shit out. Don't give yourself "just a couple of minutes" of looking at cute pictures of kittens stacked on top of each other on a hot dog bun (even though that's the cutest shit in the world and even I'm about to go look for it now), because that's procrastination. Do whatever it takes for you to avoid your distraction.

That last sentence may sound extreme, so allow me to explain this in a different way for those of you who are the cause of stupid warnings like "CAUTION: CONTAINS PEANUTS" on a jar of peanuts. If your distraction is another human being, do not murder them. Just avoid talking to them.

Postponement is ultimately your fault. It's not because you're too smart, or not challenged enough, or any of those other bullshit rationalizations you attribute to yourself in an attempt to cope with the fact that you're not changing the world with your supposed brilliance. The way the world works these days is based on drive and determination. Making things, getting stuff done, and a lack of laziness are the reasons the United States is the most productive country on the planet. That's because I've decided to replace the word "China" with "the United States." The United States manufactures more than every other nation. The United States holds a bunch of other nations' debts. I like eating United Statesmen food.

Not dilly-dallying ties in with being dependable. If you have a meeting in an hour, don't waste your fucking time, and plan out your schedule accordingly.

Let me tell you a little story of how procrastination stopped me from having a yacht. A while ago my sister and I came up with a business idea where you can pay people to do time-wasting things you can't be bothered to do. Like waiting in line at the DMV or to buy tickets, whatever. The idea never panned out because our business model included the phrase, "I don't know, pay some immigrants minimum wage or something," and, as it turned out, that wasn't very professional. Rather than taking the time to understand how to properly set up a business plan, I procrastinated and slapped it together the day of our presentation. I could've been a millionaire entrepreneur with that idea. Granted, the final draft seemed a bit slavey and read like a monster truck rally radio ad, but I still thought I had a winner.

Fine, I just made that story up, because I needed an example and I don't procrastinate that wildly. Who the hell would pay someone to stand in line for them? That's a stupid idea. Still, though, you need to avoid the pitfalls of procrastination or you could end up with one less yacht in your life. I procrastinate and I don't have a yacht. QED.

CHAPTER 32

Be Less Cynical.

"What is a cynic?
A man who knows the price of everything,
and the value of nothing."
—Oscar Wilde

I'm not gonna lie; I personally find cynical people funnier than those who aren't. There's something entertaining about someone with a bleak outlook on life shooting down the idea that everything given to us by nature is wonderful—by bringing up cancer, smallpox, polio, AIDS, leprosy, tuberculosis, etc.

With that said, there's a limit to how cynical you can be before people start making up excuses not to hang out with you. I know someone who constantly wants to party. She's one of those people who makes a plan to do something, then proceeds to hype it up incessantly until the event. Everything is, "Hell yeah, I can't wait until Friday! It's gonna be amazing!" Then, when the day comes, the event "sucks." She goes but she's bored, she can't be bothered to socialize with anyone, and she brings the mood down by talking shit about every single thing within earshot. She's the kind who's always complaining about not being able to meet guys. Then when she's at a place where she can meet hundreds of guys, she keeps her arms crossed and puts on the stankiest of stank faces. Most would call people like them "Debbie Downers." I prefer to call them idiots.

I've said before that human beings are selfish creatures, and I largely believe that. To elaborate, the human species is selfish, but selfishness on the individual scale can vary widely. There are those who look out only for themselves, those who look out for everyone, and varying degrees of everything in between. If Tyler Perry, filmmaker extraordinaire, gives a check to a charity for $1,000,000, but uses his typical "Tyler Perry Presents: Tyler Perry Gives a Check to Little Kids. A Tyler Perry Production" headline, the cynic will say he's only doing it to further his fame. Meanwhile, those little uncynical kids who just got a bunch of new books and toys don't give a fuck why he did it, just that he did it. We don't know Tyler Perry's true motivations. For all we know he's superstitious as hell and believes he has to put his name on everything or all his good luck will go away. To me, that's the only logical explanation, because A) he's lucky as hell, and B) what grown-ass man besides Donald Trump puts his name on everything he touches? Regardless, the cynic will call him out on it immediately rather than just thanking him for a good deed that hurt absolutely no one and helped many. Instead of having that level of cynicism, try being cautiously optimistic, or employ healthy skepticism.

There is a big difference between cynicism and skepticism. A cynic will doubt intent, and a skeptic will doubt veracity. To illustrate this, let's say Tyler Perry is at it again after one of his shitty movies brings in millions once more. This time he writes a check for $1,000,000 and doesn't put his name on it four or five times. The cynic will claim Tyler Perry wrote that check not to help the kids, but to help his image. The skeptic will posit that Tyler Perry didn't write that check at all, because his name only appeared on it once—it couldn't possibly be his. In this case, the cynic is a prick, and the skeptic is hilariously perceptive.

Cynicism is a byproduct of trust, or rather the lack of trust. This lack of trust is something that could either be learned through experience or inferred through a shortage of experience. If you've trusted ten strangers and been let down once, you'll probably be pretty trusting of strangers. If you've trusted three strangers and been let down twice, you probably wouldn't trust many strangers. Conversely, if you've never trusted a stranger at all, research shows you're more likely to be cynical of strangers altogether, since you have no baseline to judge them on.

The facts I gathered on that last paragraph were from some dude's blog, and I'm trusting him that he properly sourced everything and wasn't just bullshitting me.

CHAPTER 33

Show Some Interest in Politics.

"Suppose you were an idiot, and suppose you were a member of Congress; but I repeat myself."
—Mark Twain

Let's keep this short, or I'll spend four chapters ranting about Florida voters. This may come as a shock, but there's a person or group of people who pretty much decide whether or not you're allowed to partake in certain activities. Think of them as parents. Parents who, in the grand scheme of things, don't really give a flying fuck about you personally. These people are called politicians, and you should learn their names, so at the very least you can do your part in ousting them from power when they inevitably talk shit about marijuana and gay marriage.

Politicians are tasked with determining how a lot of aspects of your life will play out. You have the opportunity to choose these people, yet you squander it by selecting a goddamn color over a set of principles. Tell me, do you know your congressman's name? Your congressman is your direct representative to the federal government, and among the few politicians that'll read and respond to your mail. Those malleable fuckers will vote in favor of whatever their constituency prefers. They could be diehard, stone-cold Christians, and if ninety percent of their district wanted compulsory, ritualistic Satanic puppy sacrifice in all elementary schools across America, not only would they vote in favor of it, but they'd recite the most heartfelt speech imaginable on the Congress floor for it. When given the choice between their principles and their political seat, the majority take their seats every time. Most people forget that it's you who they answer to, and the only reason they basically get away with murder is due to their keen awareness of your political cynicism and complacency. That's why it's not unheard of for a dead politician to gain reelection.

Don't worry, though; you don't have to actively like politics. Only dickheads like politics. All you have to do is keep yourself apprised of what's going on politically, look at all sides of the story, and judge accordingly. If everyone does that shit once per year, they'll fix their country, provided it's not some autocratic clusterfuck. When it comes time to vote, pick the person who you agree with most and acts like a dickhead the least. Use your own judgment and ignore opinion reports. You hear me? Ignore opinion reports. If someone on any, and I mean any, of the major news networks tells you how they feel about something some politician did, or if anything they say includes the words "I think," stop listening. Those are merely the opinions of a couple of producers who get paid to coerce you into watching. Pay attention to news, not opinion. If you don't know the difference, just note how often they laugh on the air. (Legendary news anchorman Walter Cronkite reportedly only laughed twice in his life: when his daughter Kathy burped her name during Thanksgiving '58, and when his wife told him a dead baby joke mid-orgasm.)

That's it. That's all you have to do. You don't need to get into heated discussions, apply a bumper sticker on your car, or join a party's political circle-jerk. All you have to do is understand the talking points, make an informed decision, and yell at the television every time a commercial begins with "I'm Hugh Jassol, and I approve this message."

However, if you decide to forego giving a rat's ass about politics, when it comes time to cast a vote, please abstain.

CHAPTER 34

Go Forth, Enlightened Idiot.

> *"Real knowledge is to know
> the extent of one's ignorance."*
> —Confucius

Look at you. You're so beautiful to me now. You're like that ugly-ass baby I gave birth to, that everyone else pretends is cute just because I keep shoving photos of you down their throats.

Armed with all this newfound knowledge, perhaps you can make a change in your life. A change for the better. I'd like to offer up one more piece of advice before I let you jump out of the nest I've been nurturing you in for the past, I don't know, hour-and-a-half. Whatever. Listen up.

As you're lying in bed preparing to sleep, recap your day. Think about any of the guidelines in this book you've thoroughly violated. Think about how you can improve yourself. Think about how not being an idiot could have given you a different outcome in your day's events. Think about sex if you're a guy, because it's been seven seconds. Self-reflection is important, and the only path to Nirvana or whatever.

In middle school I forged report cards during my entire seventh-grade school year. My parents still don't know the truth. The first nine-week period, I got three Ds and three As (in math and two music classes, of course.) That was grounds for punishment, so I had to take matters into my own hands. Thanks to materials I stole from the main office, I learned to forge my own report card. I gave myself two Cs, two Bs, and two As. I actually downgraded my A in math to a B. That report card looked a lot more believable to my parents, who were aware of the contract I signed with the essence of mediocrity several years prior. I vowed to get grades of that caliber the rest of the year, and I met that goal with respectable amounts of not trying.

The problem was, I had to forge every subsequent report card I received after that, since they included grades in the previous nine-week periods. So even though I worked to get the proper grades, I ended up having to forge them anyway just to keep up the illusion of my averageness in the first nine-week period.

That event triggered something in me. It led me to understand that what I did was stupid, and simply owning up to my bad grades would've been less effort and stress in the long run. From then on, I decided I'd try to be less of an idiot. And you know what? It didn't work. I did the same shit the following year.

I'm adult, and to this day I'm irresponsible. I say inappropriate things at inappropriate times. I'll eat something that has fallen on the floor and later wonder out-loud why it burned like Lucifer's breath when I shat. I've used the little flashlight on my keychain to look for my keys. But I'm working on it, and so should you. Just be aware of yourself and how your behavior affects others, or your relationship with your own head.

I guess what I'm trying to say is, "Cease thy infernal buffoonery!"

ACKNOWLEDGMENTS

In writing this book, I sought the help of some wonderful people, and I would like to take a quick moment to recognize their contributions with as few snarky jokes as my mind will allow.

I would like to express my sincere thanks to my main, top-dog proofreaders: Dana, Melissa, Megan, and Vivian. Without their suggestions and critiques this book may have ended up with nine chapters dedicated to defecation jokes, rather than just the one.

The help of my editor DeAnna and cover artist Ashley is also greatly appreciated. If you're a fan of the low-to-nil number of grammatical errors and spelling mistakes, check DeAnna out at deannaknippling.com. As for Ashley, everyone judges books by their covers—let's not kid ourselves here—so find her at clevercovers.net.

Thanks to Amanda for the pen name. Sure, current web searches for "Orlando Winters" produce mostly climate reports, but one day I'll be at the forefront.

Thank you, Wikipedia, greatest thing ever.

Also, a big thanks to Enrique Iglesias for creating truly horrendous music not at all pleasing to the ears in any capacity whatsoever.

And lastly, thanks to my amazing parents for not giving up on unprotected sex after their first child. That must've been tough. Kids can be so annoying.

ABOUT THE AUTHOR

Orlando Winters is a Miami-based critic of all things, with a propensity for stream-of-consciousness ranting and irrelevant segues. That pretty much sums everything up nicely.

Read his blog: boywritesmiami.com

Printed in Great Britain
by Amazon